THE PLAY'S THE THING

A GAME OF SHAKESPEAREAN
PLAYWRIGHTS AND ACTORS
BY MARK TRUMAN OF MAGPIE GAMES

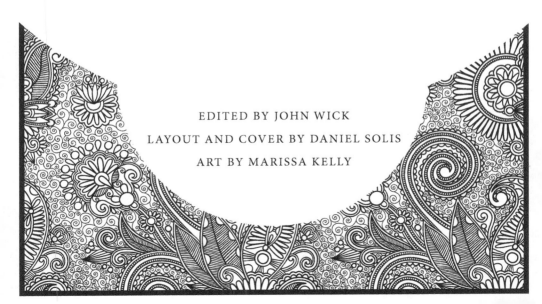

EDITED BY JOHN WICK
LAYOUT AND COVER BY DANIEL SOLIS
ART BY MARISSA KELLY

ISBN 978-0-9848293-0-9

Aspects are from the Fate System, designed by Fred Hicks and Rob Donoghue. Great thanks to both of them for making roleplaying a better hobby for everyone.

If you'd like to create additional materials for use with *The Play's The Thing*, we would love to hear from you. Email us at *info@magpiegames.com*.

First Printing: February 2012

WE ARE SUCH STUFF
AS DREAMS ARE MADE ON;

AND OUR LITTLE LIFE
IS ROUNDED WITH A SLEEP.

– Prospero, *The Tempest*, Act 4, Scene 1

DEDICATION

To Debi Kierst, who first opened my eyes to the greatness in all of us. Everything I have done in my life since high school has been because you taught me to reach for greatness, no matter my age.

THANKS TO...

James Bronaugh, Austin Cox, Pete Figtree, Derrick Kapchinsky, Eloy Lasanta, Steve Randazzo, Lara Rosner, Ryan Ross, Theresa Strike, Jason Pitre, Paul Truman, Nathan Wallwork, Jonathan Walton, Ben Woerner, all of our playtesters and typo-hunters, the insightful members of the Indie Game Developer Network, the wonderful folks at story-games.com, my editor, John Wick, and everyone else that I've ever talked with about the game. Thank you all for making this game possible.

Special thanks also to our Shakespearean Consultant, Christina Scott Sayer Grey. Without you, this book would be far less true to the Bard's words, and far less educational for the Players. Thank you.

And to all our Backers: "I can no other answer make, but, thanks, and thanks."

THE PLAYBILL

Thank you to all our Kickstarter backers who made *The Play's The Thing* possible. From Globe Groundlings to Elder Patrons, your support helped this project grow and evolve into the book you hold today. Thank you.

The Globe Groundling
Justin Rogers

Globe Gentry
A-Bomb & G-Girl
Anders Smith
Asa MacDermott
Cheryl Trooskin-Zoller
Christian Opperer
Christine Thompson
Christopher 'Halaku' Buser
Christopher Lipinski
CS Hearns
Dan Bongert

David Miessler-Kubanek
Dumon
Ellen Kaye-Cheveldayoff
Evil Hat Productions
Heath Holmes
J. Peters
Jay Shaffstall
Jenny Moser Jurling
John Colagioia
Jonathan Walton
Josh Rensch
Joshua Kubli
Kirt Dankmyer
Lauren D. Rogers

Lester Smith

Lester Ward

Manuel Marron

Martin Bell

Paolo Busi

Pete Griffith

R Rees

Reverance Pavane

Rhys Harrison

Sean Dornan-Fish

Shane Mclean

Sir Matthew

Steven K. Watkins

Theresa Strike

Tim Morgan

Tim Rodriguez

Treena Shapiro

Tresi Arvizo

W. "Shaman" Obenshain

Xavier Aubuchon-Mendoza

Yolgie

Zachary Hall

Globe Nobles

Amanda Giles

Christina Scott Sayer Grey

Daniel Koyata

Meera Barry

Supporting Actors of the Globe

Adam Boisvert

Adam Rajski

Aleksander R. N. Rødner

Alex Strang

Alexander Tigwell

Alf Whitehead

Allison D Hicks

Amber Mahoney

Amy Waller

Andrew & Anna McColl

Andrew Robertson

Austin Stanley

Brad Tuggle

Brian Engard

Caitlin Smith

Cameron Goble

Cameron Hays

Cat Davidson-Hall

Chris Nolen

Chris Whissen

Christopher Fee

Christopher Robichaud

Colin O'Kelley

Daisy Farnum

Darcey & Adam Wunker

David 'Doc Blue' Wendt

David A Hill Jr

David Bennett

David Gallo

David Morgans

David Wilhelm

Donnelle Fuller

Dr U Kadolsky

Edward Sagritalo

Ellen Forsyth

ELOY LASANTA

emanchar

Erik Myers

Eva R. Sarachan

Flavio Mortarino

Franz Georg Roesel

Heidi McIver

Herman Duyker

Irven Keppen

Jack Gulick

James Gabrielsen

Jason Corley

Jason Kinzer

Jason Vanhee

JC Cohen

Jennifer Steen

Jeremy Kostiew

Jeremy Melloul

Jim Reader

Jim Sweeney

Jimmy Kayne Newell

John and Jackie Skotnik

Jonathan "Buddha" Davis

Jonathan Jordan

Joseph Terranova

Josh Crowe

Josh Lee

Julia Ellingboe

Jussi Myllyluoma

Katie Harwood

Keith Fyans

Kelley Barnes

kelly van campen

Kit La Touche

Kristina Golubiewski

Leslie Furlong

Lukas Matthews

Marc Kevin Hall

Mario Dongu

Matthew McFarland

Maureen Singleton

Meguey Baker

Melissa Schumacher

Michael Goldman

Michael Harnish

Michael Richards

Michelle Micheo

Mick Bradley

Monica Thomas

Nathan Wallwork

Nathaniel Garth

Rich Rogers

Robby Anderson

Robert Daley

Rose T. Diaz

Sarah Bowman

Scott Underwood- Chicagoland Games

Stephanie Franklin

Stephanie Turner

Steve Gooch

Strahinja Acimovic

Tawnly Pranger

Ted Corley

Tom Shortridge

Tristan Robert

Victor Wyatt

Virginia Morris

Warren Sistrom

Lead Actors of the Globe

Arc Dream Publishing

C. Robert Stevens

Cathleen Cole

Emma Camilleri

Fred Barry

J. Derrick Kapchinsky

Jason Ramboz

Jeffrey "Prospero" Wong

Jenny Bennett

Jody Kline

John Mehrholz

Joseph Streeky

Junius "Stoney" Stone

Kat L.

Katherine Schramm

Kent Plumb

Marguerite Kenner and Alasdair Stuart

Michael Webb
Phillip Bailey
PJ Saad
Randy & Charlene Truman
Simon Ward
Simon Withers
Julio "Morgan Blackhand" Escajedo
Steve Dempsey
Terrence "Terentius" Micheau
Tom Cadorette

Prima Donnas of the Globe
Daniel Stanke
Jason Pitre
Noah McBrayer Jones

Elder Patrons of the Globe
Dhaunae De Vir
Lori Herrin
Paul Tevis
Sean Doonan

CONTENTS

INTRODUCTION

WELCOME TO *THE PLAY'S THE THING*

Hello! My name is Mark, and this is my roleplaying game, *The Play's The Thing*. I originally wrote this game for a weeklong competition called Game Chef. I was given one week to come up with a 3,000 word, original roleplaying game centered around the 2011 theme: William Shakespeare. I knew right away that I wanted to capture my experience as a high school thespian, where the relationship between Actors and Playwrights was a fascinating drama that played out on top of the plays we produced. I also knew that I wanted it to be a game where the players took direct control of the narrative, and made interesting changes to Shakespeare's work.

In this revised and expanded version of the game, you'll get the chance to play famous roles with your friends, to demand more time on stage as an Actor, to try to rein in your Actors as a Playwright, and to create incredible new stories based on the works of William Shakespeare. And while you'll be encouraged to play along with the themes and motifs of The Play that the Playwright picks, each and every Actor will have a chance to rip up the script and make The Bard's works even better.

If you're totally confused about what a roleplaying game is keep reading and I'll explain how it works. If you'd like to see an example, visit www.magpiegames.com/theplayreplay and you can read through a replay of an actual game session.

If you're an experienced player, and you're ready to get started, skip to page 19 for the rules on creating your Actor.

If you're an experienced storyteller, and you want tips on how to make the most of the game, skip to page 57 for the Playwright section.

If you have played *The Play's The Thing* before, skip to page 73 for Scripts you can use while playing the game, or page 120 for the Quick Start Guide.

Break a leg!

If you're brand new to roleplaying games, I'm really glad you picked up this book. If you know anything about Magpie Games, the company I founded with Marissa Kelly—my partner, illustrator, and girlfriend—you should know that we are incredibly interested in bringing new people into gaming. We love roleplaying and we're eager to share it with you.

But what is it? What is roleplaying?

In short, it's improvisational acting with rules. You and your friends create characters—from your own imaginations—and the game gives you some rules for how your characters can interact with each other and with the setting. In this game, those characters are Actors. (You can read more about The Actors on page 19.) It may seem silly when you first start speaking as your character, but once you get the hang of it you and your friends can create amazing stories together.

In most cases, one of your friends will be responsible for keeping track of the rules and weaving everyone's contributions into a single story. In this game, we call the referee/storyteller The Playwright. It's The Playwright's job to keep The Play running smoothly, and to interpret the rules if there's any disagreement. (You can read more about The Playwright on page 57.) Playing as The Playwright can be a lot of fun; it's neat to see your friends play out the ideas you bring to the table.

Overall, the whole thing is like playing Cowboys and Indians; everyone knows that we're just pretending, but that doesn't make the drama any less real. You and your friends will laugh and cry and hope and dream, all because you will create characters who will take on a lives of their own within the game. A great roleplaying session, like a great movie or book, makes you forget about the rest of the world, and it's bittersweet when the story comes to a close.

THE BIG THREE QUESTIONS

I'm a big fan of game designer Jared Sorensen's Big Three Questions, a set of inquiries that all designers should answer when trying to design a new game. These questions help me focus the process and make sure that the game isn't just a rehash of a tired concept or a jumbled mess of rules. Here are my answers to the Big Three Questions for *The Play's The Thing*:

WHAT IS MY GAME ABOUT?

My game is about the dramatic conflict between the Playwright and Actors when producing a Shakespearean play. While it may seem to the audience that a finished play is merely actors reading lines, anyone who has been a part of a production knows that the rehearsal process is as much about what the Actors add as it is about what the Playwright has written.

In my game, the players portray Actors who have been called by the Playwright to rehearse a Tragedy, Comedy, or History. The Actors must follow the style, plot, and lines they are given, but will, of course, attempt to improve the play by offering their own suggestions and improvising as often as they can get away with it.

The Playwright, on the other hand, wishes to see his work brought to life by the Actors, but is bound by their egos, desires, and failings. He must inspire them to greatness, and cannot let them derail the entire show. He has to use their new ideas to improve the show without ruining what made the show great in the first place.

How does my game do that?

My game captures the divine, messy art of the theater by focusing on the contest of wills between the Playwright and the Actors.

At the opening, The Playwright lays out the general plot of each Act of the play, casts the Actors in Parts and Plots, and gives each of them a few lines that they must say during a scene. The Actors may make changes to the story as it is being told, adding new conflicts and characters to make the play more interesting and their Parts more important.

What behaviors does my game punish or reward?

My game rewards players for playing their Part in keeping with the type of play selected by the Playwright. Each joke in a Comedy or misunderstanding in a Tragedy will earn "story points" from the Playwright that can be used to make changes to the narrative. Thus, those who play along with the Playwright at first will find that they can influence the story later, perhaps altering the play tremendously.

STORY POINTS

So what are story points? Some games track hit points or mana points to tell you how much health or magical ability a character has available in a scene. In *The Play's The Thing*, I've tried to keep things simple; you won't have to track any of that stuff. All of the Actors have some statistics that describe their abilities, but no one in your Troupe is actually out to hurt or kill any other member of the acting group. Hopefully.

But your Playwright can reward you for playing along with the themes of The Play he or she has selected by giving you story points. Those points, usually poker chips or small tokens, can be spent to affect The Play, to activate your character's abilities, and to bribe other players into going along with your plans. Think of them as an out-of-character currency, units that you can spend to do what you want in the game.

One of the first questions that players ask is "Do we have to play in the Elizabethan era? Do we have to pretend to be pretentious actors who perform for the common people while rich nobles sit in the box seats and pretend to fit in?"

Nope. But you might find that fun. And if your gaming group feels that the setting should be Elizabethan, go for it. It can be a blast for your Playwright to pretend to be Shakespeare, for your Actors to put on their English accents, and for your whole Troupe to experience what it was like to read *King Lear* for the first time.

But if you want to play a group of Actors in the 1920s, or the 1950s, or the modern day, that's fine too. *The Play's The Thing* is a set of rules that help you explore how Actors and Playwrights work together to produce great plays. You can make that work in any era, with any group of actors, about any play. It's up to all of you to pick the era that would be the most fun.

WHAT'S INCLUDED HERE

To help you play *The Play's the Thing*, I've included:

- ✦ Rules for creating Actors, including lists of Parts, Plots, Places, and Props
- ✦ Rules for playing *The Play's The Thing* for Actors and Playwrights
- ✦ Guidance for Playwrights on how to run game sessions

If you're interested in downloading additional resources, including Alternate Scripts and errata, visit www.magpiegames.com/theplay for more downloads.

WHAT YOU'LL NEED

In order to play *The Play's The Thing*, you'll need:

- ✦ More than ten six-sided dice
- ✦ A few pens or pencils
- ✦ A few blank notecards
- ✦ Three to six friends

THE ACTORS

To start, each player should create an Actor to portray for the session. While your Troupe may be putting on a production of Hamlet, you're not actually playing a character from The Play. Instead, you're going to portray an Actor who wants to get… well, whatever Actors hope to get out of being in a show!

You could be…

… the diva who hopes to get the biggest part she can get with the most number of lines and the largest spotlight.

… the character actor who hopes to land an interesting part that will further cement his reputation as a quirky, mercurial thespian.

… the layabout who pretends to care, but really just wants to do as little acting as possible while still getting paid.

… the method actor who respects the craft and hopes to get the role that is the most challenging to portray well.

Regardless, it's your job to think up a thespian to play during the session. Give your Actor a name and a background appropriate to whatever time period your Troupe agrees upon. Make sure to note both on your character sheet, and share your story with the rest of your Troupe. After all, you've probably all been acting together for some time.

In addition, you should write your Actor's name on the front of your nameplate and your real name on the back. This will help your gaming group learn the Actors' names quickly, and when you're talking out of character (as yourself), you can flip your nameplate around to display your real name so that people know that you aren't speaking as your Actor.

A Rose By Any Other Name…

Having trouble thinking of a name? Use your middle name as a first name, and the street you lived on as a kid as your last name. For example, my "actor name" would be Diaz Monroe and Marissa's "actor name" would be Michaella Auburn.

Actors have three stats, ranging from one to three, which represent their Acting Chops: Logos, Pathos, and Ethos. Each player has a total pool of six points to place in Acting Chops, but each Chop is capped at three points.

Logos represents an Actor's verbal acumen and control over the events of the Play. Actors with high Logos scores can convince the Playwright to alter the course of the narrative, rewriting the outcome of events.

Pathos represents an Actor's emotional resonance and control over the other characters in the Play. Actors with high Pathos scores are superb at manipulating the emotions of other Actors and the Playwright, changing Parts and Plots that involve other characters.

Ethos represents an Actor's narrative understanding and control over the setting of the Play. Actors with high Ethos scores are good at manipulating Places and Props, often using details in the environment to convince the Playwright to change the setting.

Go ahead and put points into each of the stats on your character sheet. Remember that no individual Chop can be higher than three.

Acting Chops are the basis for all the rolls you will make for your character during the play. If you want your character to be good at manipulating a specific part of the play, such as the Props on stage or the relationships characters have with each other, make sure to put the points in the appropriate Chop.

In addition to Chops, Actors also have a Type. While no two Actors are identical, Types represent the kind of character the Actor is often cast to play. Someone who is usually cast as a Villain may try to play a noble king, but old habits die hard and the audience expects you to live up to your reputation.

Each Type has two abilities, one "Onstage" and one "Offstage." The Onstage ability is used to affect events when the Actor is on the stage, playing his part. The Offstage ability, on the other hand, can only be used when the Actor is waiting in the wings, hovering offstage and hoping to get back into the spotlight. Most of these abilities require the use of a story point (see page 15 for more on story points).

You should choose one Type for your Actor. Your Type can change over time—a particularly perfect performance of a certain role can earn you a new reputation—but only if the Playwright and fellow Actors approve the change at the end of a play. For now, whatever Type you choose is the reputation you currently own; it won't change during The Play the Playwright has selected.

All Actor Types are gender-neutral; some of the best Ingénues are men, and some of the best hams are women. Also, remember that Types describe only your actor, not the roles your actor will be playing. It's totally possible for a Villain Actor to end up playing Hamlet, or a Lead Actor to end up playing Iago.

Direction

Each Type also has a Direction, an action that the Actor must take when the Playwright directs them to do so. No matter the cost, the Actors must follow Direction when the Playwright calls for it. The Playwright, however, may only Direct an Actor once per Act of The Play.

"The actor should be able to create the universe in the palm of his hand"
—Sir Laurence Olivier

Famous Examples: Judi Dench, Patrick Stewart, Helen Mirren, John
Barrymore

The Lead is the professional actor, the thespian most likely to win awards and draw crowds. He may be a diva, but the Troupe respects his talent. Even when he is not playing the lead role, he beguiles his audience with a deep and complex portrayal of a character that they only thought they knew…and will never see the same way again.

The Lead, more often than not, takes his job seriously. After all, he didn't get good at stagecraft by watching other people act. He's been in quite a few shows, knows his way around the theatre, and tries to act in a manner befitting an artist of the highest order.

That said, he's not a complete dud. A good number of famous lead actors are also notorious pranksters or showmen. They aren't above getting their hands dirty to keep things interesting on the set, and know how to get the Playwright to give them enough leeway to keep the show from falling to dull mediocrity.

- *Onstage Ability:* The Lead knows how to act with subtle skill. You may spend a story point to bring an additional Part to an Act beyond the limits of your Logos.

- *Offstage Ability:* The Lead knows how to bolster morale. You may spend story points on behalf of another Actor who has run out of story points.

- *Direction:* At the Playwright's request, the Lead must stand and face a threat even though he may wish to leave the stage.

"*Acting is the expression of a neurotic impulse. It's a bum's life. The principal benefit acting has afforded me is the money to pay for my psychoanalysis.*"
—*Marlon Brando*

Famous Examples: Kenneth Branaugh, Glenn Close, Laurence Fishburne, Richard Burton

While some would describe him as clumsy, The Ham is often the most exciting and interesting Actor in the Play. He knows how to turn a phrase, get the laugh, and move the crowd, all with the utmost energy and charm. Even roles that seem too serious or too small become magical in the hands of the Ham, prompting audiences to rethink why they "never thought that part was funny" or "never imagined that role could be moving."

For what the Ham gives up in skill, he gains in energy and charisma. He best stands alone on stage and commands the audience's attention in a soliloquy; he alone can make the audience burst out laughing at a well-timed pratfall or ironic aside. The Ham is always aware of the audience, and he loves the attention.

In fact, he probably loves the attention too much. While other Actors are content to sit offstage and wait for their cue, The Ham is always a heartbeat away from returning to the stage. After all, the audience is waiting...

- ✦ *Onstage Ability:* The Ham knows how to play up his part. You may yell "Cut" without spending a story point.
- ✦ *Offstage Ability:* The Ham knows how to get on stage. You may spend a story point to compel another Actor to call for your character.
- ✦ *Direction:* At the Playwright's request, The Ham must perform a Soliloquy.

"I think if you do something effectively, whether you're the lover or the comic or the action guy or the villain like I play, movies are very expensive to make. Chances are you'll get asked to play that part again."
—Christopher Walken

Famous Examples: Conrad Veidt, Erick Avari, Helena Bonham-Carter

The Villain reeks of villainy and deceit. When she walks on stage, the crowd lets out a quiet hiss, as if to remind her that they do not trust her. They know that regardless of The Villain's role, she will turn against the hero, and it will end in bloodshed and agony. At best, she will be defeated in the final scene, laid to rest by the righteous forces of good.

On the other hand, everyone knows her name.

It's not easy to be The Villain, to know that the audience expects you to do awful things to perfectly nice people. But she finds that betrayal, violence, and treachery come so easily to her that the audience's expectations are simply second nature. The Villain is who she is, and to pretend otherwise is not worth her time.

- *Onstage Ability:* The Villain knows how to destroy other characters. You may spend a story point to Poison or Wound another character without a roll.
- *Offstage Ability:* The Villain knows the cruel potential of a whispered word. You may spend a story point to whisper a nasty rumor to a character present in an ongoing scene. You may spend another story point to make them believe the rumor is true.
- *Direction:* At the Playwright's request, The Villain must deny a plea for mercy or justice, turning a cold heart to even the most reasonable of requests.

"There are some great roles —mostly in Shakespeare's tragedies—which no one can play at full strength from beginning to end. One simply hopes that one can hit the peaks as often as one has the strength."
—*Dame Peggy Ashcroft*

Famous Examples: Elizabeth Barry, Kate Winslet, Olivia Hussey, Jimmy Stewart

Virginal and naive, The Ingénue has the unforced heart of a child. Others wish to shield her from the world, but she knows that her innocence is fleeting, that her sorrow and joy are all the more precious because they are ephemeral.

Typically The Ingénue is relatively new to the world of acting, and not well acquainted with the other Actors in the Troupe. On occasion, however, some Actors manage to keep their unworldly ways safe, and continue to project the naive charm that makes The Ingénue unique. It is a function of outlook, not age.

For the most part, The Ingénue is not stupid or careless, but trusting and good-natured. She finds herself in trouble not because she can't see it coming, but because she can't imagine that someone would truly mean her harm. The Ingénue, in many ways, represents what is best about humanity, and she connects with the audience on that level.

- *Onstage Ability:* The Ingénue knows how to win hearts. You may spend a story point to reroll a failed Pathos roll.
- *Offstage Ability:* The Ingénue can inspire greatness. You may spend a story point to allow another character to reroll a failed Logos roll.
- *Direction:* At the Playwright's request, The Ingénue must place herself in danger.

Now that you've placed your points in Acting Chops and selected your Acting Type, you're done! You'll select Parts, Plots, and Props later, once your Playwright has explained which play you'll be performing and what roles will be available. You can read all about that in The Play.

In the meantime, go ahead and talk with the other Actors about what kind of background ties you might already have. Have you worked together before? Do you like being an actor? What shows have you previously done? While most of this game takes place during a busy rehearsal, it's good to have some sense of what your relationships with the other actors have been like before we open the curtain.

Just don't ever tell them "Good Luck…"

THE PLAY

If you've ever been in a real Troupe, you know that assigning parts can be a wild and crazy process. All the Actors want to land the perfect part, but no one wants to commit too early. In *The Play's The Thing*, you'll have to compete with your fellow Actors to get the Part you want, all the while trying to make sure that the story has elements you like.

Once the players have built their Actors, the Playwright starts the session by introducing The Play. The Playwright may choose to produce a known Shakespearean play, but can also choose to produce a new work he or she has "written." Regardless, The Playwright should give a short synopsis that summarizes the Play, hand out the Cast List, and give five story points to each player.

The Playwright casts the play by offering up a Name for one of the Characters, a Part (King, Exile, etc), a Plot (Daughter, Forsworn, etc), and a Prop (Coin, Sword, Crown) with a story point reward — usually two to three story points — for the Actor who accepts the role. Usually I do this by writing the Character's name at the top of an index card and listing the starting Part and Plot underneath the name.

The Actors then have a few options:

- Bid up the story point reward by adding Parts and Plots to the character
- Claim the character to get the story points bid so far
- Pass on the Character

To determine the order of play, all the players roll a single d6. The highest roll goes first, then bidding, claiming, or passing continues in a clockwise order. Ties go to the youngest player. Players may either claim the part or bid on the part and cannot do both. If players have already claimed a part, they cannot claim another and must only bid or pass.

Types of Plays

Remember that you can earn Story Points for fitting your actions and dialogue to the type of play being produced. Here are some tips for each type:

COMEDY—These plays are typified by romantic adventures between highborn characters who are amused by the slapstick humor of lower-class buffoons. You'll get story points if you play the noble lovers with romantic zeal or the common comedic characters with lewd wit.

TRAGEDY—These plays always end in death. Lots of it. Mostly on stage. You'll get story points if you play your characters as driven, but flawed, unintentionally driving all of the cast members toward a bloody and deadly end.

HISTORY—These plays center on the rise or fall of titular character, like the conquering hero Henry in Henry V. You'll get story points when you make nationalistic speeches, attempt to establish your dynasty by taking the throne, or lead troops on the battlefield with courage and nobility.

Since all of Shakespeare's works were adapted from well-known sources, The Playwright isn't the only one who gets to define the elements of the Characters. The Actors can add new Parts, Plots, and Props to Characters by spending a story point and saying "I know this story!" Add the Part or Plot to the index card, and place the story point with the rest of the points already set out by the Actors and the Playwright.

For example, an Actor may say "I know this story! The Ruler is also a Witch!" or "I know this story! The Father of Ophelia is also the Father of Laertes!" It's not necessary for these additions to be true to the original script. Sometimes it's fun to turn Othello and Iago into brothers or to transform Romeo and Juliet into Faerie creatures. Keep in mind that the point of the game is to break the rules!

The "I know this story!" process results in Characters who will have more than one Part or Plot, but are undeniably Shakespearean creations. A few examples:

King Lear: The Ruler, Father to Cordelia, Wears a Crown

Earl of Kent: The Knight, The Exile, The Hero, Sworn to Lear, Wears a Sword

Cordelia: The Maiden, Friend to the Fool, Daughter to Lear, Holds a Standard

Don't worry if something doesn't get added to a Character before an Actor claims it. There are plenty of chances to add new Elements (Plots, Parts, and Props) to Characters once The Play starts.

Adding or Removing Elements to the Play

Actors may gain (or lose) Parts, Plots, and Props as the play progresses. The Playwright can assign (or remove) new elements by spending a story point or Actors may suggest such changes as a Major Edit.

CHAPTER 3

The first actor to claim a Character gets the story points bid by the Playwright and other Actors for that role up to that point. If no Actor wants a Character (i.e. you go around the circle twice and no one claims), the Playwright claims that role, and all the story points are lost to the Actors. If that Character is needed during The Play, the Playwright will portray it.

Anyone can take any role the Playwright proposes, even if it seems like a strange match based on the Actor's Type. In fact, it's fun to see Hamlet played by The Villain or Richard III played by the Ingénue. Part of the magic of *The Play's The Thing* is the crazy, mixed-up stories that come from altering Shakespeare's works. Don't ruin the fun by trying to plan anything out as you bid up and claim roles.

And since The Bard had to cast his women as boys who dressed up as girls, your Troupe can have any gender play any part. One of the first playtesting sessions I ran featured Kate from *Taming of the Shrew*...played by my friend Nate. Nate tackled one of Shakespeare's famous ladies with gusto, and his portrayal added a lot to the story. Don't be afraid to cross genders!

In short, the Actors should focus only on the roles they want, unconstrained by the Actor's gender, age, or Type. After all, you're Acting!

Too Many Parts

If you have more parts than you have actors, the Playwright can "read" for the Characters who were not cast.

Parts are the formal roles that the Actors embody on the stage. They represent the jobs and titles that the Characters possess, and are usually the focus of the Play. A Character may have a number of Parts with different jobs, titles, and responsibilities jockeying for priority in the Character's story.

In a Shakespearean production, Parts are incredibly important. The roles Characters play in society, and the way those roles shape the human experience, are a topic that rises again and again in Shakespeare's work. In other words, Actors care a lot about Parts because they determine quite a bit about how their skills will be used in the production.

Each Part has two features: an Invoke and a Compel. Anyone who has played the FATE game system should be familiar with these, but for those of you who aren't, here's a quick guide:

Actors can Invoke their Parts when attempting to convince the Playwright that a change should be made because it fits the role the Actor has in The Play. For example:

> *"I think The Knight should defend the Maiden successfully instead of allowing her to be taken by the bandits. He made a promise to help her get home safely."*

Each time that the Actor Invokes his Part, it costs one story point—which goes to The Playwright—and gets the Actor two dice. We'll discuss how the dice work soon (See Edit Mechanics on page 52), but more dice is always a good thing when trying to convince The Playwright to make a change.

At the same time, The Playwright and other Actors can Compel an Actor to keep in line with a Part during The Play. For example:

> *"I think the Knight should murder his friend because his liege ordered him to do so."*

Like an Invoke, a Compel costs the person tagging it. In this case, it costs two story points to tag it—which go to the Compelled Actor. If he or she spends one story point, however, the Actor being Compelled can resist the Compel, but receives no story points. Any story points used to resist a Compel go to The Playwright, regardless of who tried to Compel the Actor.

 LIST OF PARTS

The Ruler

You are lord of a kingdom or a commander of men. Others respect your rule, but may want to unseat you to claim power.

- *Invoke:* Gain two dice when you are performing your duties.
- *Compel:* You cannot conceal your true identity.

The Exile

You have been cast from your home. You may wish to go home, but either cannot find your way or are forbidden to return.

- *Invoke:* Gain two dice when acting against those who caused your exile.
- *Compel:* You are alien to this place. Act like it.

The Maiden

You are the prize to be won. You may be poised to inherit a kingdom or be blessed with extraordinary beauty. Regardless, others seek your hand.

- *Invoke:* Gain two dice when dealing with those who want you.
- *Compel:* Your position is weak. You must not trust others.

The Fool

You are a source of amusement for Lords and Ladies. Only you have the ability to safely opine in the presence of the powerful.

- *Invoke:* Gain two dice when you speak truth to power.
- *Compel:* You must make lords laugh to keep your head.

The Hero

You stand for righteous justice. While you may not always choose wisely, your heart is pure.

- *Invoke:* Gain two dice when defending another character.
- *Compel:* You cannot let evil go unpunished.

The Knight

You have sworn yourself to service of a land, ruler, or ideal. You may not have chosen this path willingly, but you follow it with honor.

- *Invoke:* Gain two dice when honoring your commitments.
- *Compel:* You cannot act against your liege's will.

The Nurse

You have raised the sons and daughters of others. Your charges cannot help but be influenced your words.

- *Invoke:* Gain two dice when dealing with those you have raised.
- *Compel:* You are not brave, cautioning safety always.

The Witch

You have given yourself over to the wilds of nature. You seek balance in chaos and truth in dreams.

- *Invoke:* Gain two dice when you serve the lords of nature.
- *Compel:* You cannot allow men to conquer the wilds.

The Faerie

You are a creature from the world of the Fae. You may pass as human, but you know that you are not like the other mortals.

- *Invoke:* Gain two dice when dealing with Faerie magic.
- *Compel:* You are bound by secret contracts. Honor them.

The Commoner

You are a member of the common class of men and women. Your life promises to be short, brutal, and full of hard work.

- *Invoke:* Gain two dice when you navigate the world of the lower classes.
- *Compel:* You are hardened to the ways of the world. The suffering of others does not concern you.

PLOTS

Plots represent relationships, containing both a descriptor (Betrayer, Sworn, Daughter) and a focus on another Character. The focus of a Plot must actually be in the Play; players cannot use a Plot centered on a Character who will not ever appear onstage. Just like Parts, Plots are not mutually exclusive; a Character may have a number of different Plots at one time.

Keep in mind that Plots are not mutual unless both Characters have the Plot on their sheets. If a Plot is one-sided, it merely indicates that one Character is unaware of the relationship, or purposefully ignores it. It's up to the Actors to work that detail out between themselves.

As with Parts, Actors can Invoke their Plots when attempting to convince the Playwright that a change should be made because it fits the relationships attached to a Character. For example:

"I think King Lear should forgive Cordelia because she is his Daughter."

Each time that the Actor Invokes his Plot, it costs one story point—which goes to The Playwright—and gets the Actor two dice. We'll discuss how the dice work soon (See Edit Mechanics on page 52), but more dice is always a good thing when trying to convince The Playwright to make a change.

At the same time, The Playwright and other Actors can Compel an Actor to keep in line with a Plot during The Play. For example:

"I think King Lear should ignore the Earl of Kent's advice because he trusts his Daughters, Reagan and Goneril."

Like an Invoke, a Compel costs the person tagging it. In this case, it costs two story points to tag it—which go to the Compelled Actor. If he or she spends one story point, however, the Actor being Compelled can resist the Compel, but receives no story points. Any story points used to resist a Compel go to The Playwright, regardless of who tried to Compel the Actor.

Son / Daughter

You are the child of another character in the Play. Your parentage may be secret or you may hate and loathe your parents, but the bonds of kin are not to be disregarded.

- *Invoke:* Gain two dice when dealing with your parents.
- *Compel:* You must obey the head of your family, ignoring your own desires.

Mother / Father

One of the characters in the Play is your child. You see in your scion too much of yourself.

- *Invoke:* Gain two dice when dealing with your son or daughter.
- *Compel:* You cannot harm your progeny, physically or emotionally, even if it would help them.

Brother / Sister

You are the sibling of another character in the Play. Your feelings about this relationship may vary, but you know he or she is kin.

- *Invoke:* Gain two dice when dealing with your sibling.
- *Compel:* You cannot betray your brother or sister, no matter how much they have hurt you.

In Love

You are madly, insanely, truly in love with another character in the Play. There are no words to express the depth of your emotions.

- *Invoke:* Gain two dice when pursuing your true love.
- *Compel:* Love burns like a fire in your heart. Act the fool for it.

Sworn

You have sworn an oath of service to another character in the Play. This oath may compel your constant servitude or merely keep you from a particular course of action.

- *Invoke:* Gain two dice when obeying the oath your swore.
- *Compel:* Your loyalty goes beyond your oath. Follow your liege even when dismissed from your service.

Betrayer

You have turned against a character in the Play who trusts you deeply. Your betrayal has already gone too far to be forgiven.

- *Invoke:* Gain two dice when hurting the one who trusts you.
- *Compel:* You want your victim to know what you've done.

Enemy

You hate another character in the Play for crimes, injustices, and betrayals that have gone on too long to be rectified. You seek nothing less than complete and total victory.

- *Invoke:* Gain two dice when attempting to destroy your enemy.
- *Compel:* You cannot see the forest for the trees. Strike blindly and without forethought.

Pawn

You serve another character in the Play, but not by choice. Instead, your master has tricked, misled, or blackmailed you into his or her service.

- *Invoke:* Gain two dice when completing your master's bidding.
- *Compel:* Pawns are weak and easily misled. Screw something up.

Rival

You have a longstanding rivalry with another character in the Play. You may respect your adversary, but you do everything in your power to trump him or her.

- *Invoke:* Gain two dice when attempting to surpass your rival.
- *Compel:* You cannot let your rival win. Pursue victory, no matter the cost.

Friend

You have a close friendship with another character in the Play. While you may not always see eye to eye with him or her, you are quick to come to your friend's aid.

- *Invoke:* Gain two dice when helping your friend accomplish a task.
- *Compel:* You must protect your friend from harm, even if it puts you in danger.

PROPS

Props are items that the Actors bring on stage for dramatic effect. Props are not unique, and two Actors can both have the same kind of Prop on stage at the same time. Characters rarely start with Props, but they may be created during play or given to a Character by the Playwright. Each Prop adds a free die to an appropriate roll.

 LIST OF PROPS

Knife
Add one die when Wounding another character.

Poison
Add one die when Poisoning another character

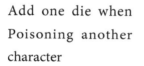
Letter
Add one die when spreading secrets.

Disguise
Add one die when hiding in plain sight.

Lantern
Add one die when exploring a new Set.

Crown
Add one die when acting as the rightful ruler of a kingdom.

Sword
Add one die when participating in a duel.

Standard
Add one die when leading an army against your enemies.

Coin
Add one die when convincing another to follow your plan.

For each Act in the play, the Playwright will specify a Set that the Actors have to use. The Sets are broad and general, conveying to the Audience only the most general details about the Act. A Nature Set might be represented by a few trees scattered about the stage, while a Palace Set will likely have brightly colored walls and a few guards.

Places are details given to a Set in order to add more information to an Act in the Play. A Palace Set, for example, might be the location of a Formal Court or an Extravagant Party, features of the Act that will help the Characters create more interesting scenes.

As with Parts and Plots, there is no limit to the number of Places that can exist in a Set; each Place can take up a bit of room on the stage for itself or overlap with an existing set if they aren't in direct conflict. Players and Playwrights should feel free to add custom Places in order to flesh out the bare bones set established by the Playwright when laying out the Act.

Unlike Plots and Parts, Places are not fixed to one Character, nor do they require story points to use. Instead, any character can add a die to a roll based on an appropriate Place for free. For example:

"I think King Lear should banish Reagan and Goneril. After all, this is a Formal Court and their treachery has been exposed."

Nature Set

Cloaked in mystery, Nature is the wild darkness hovering just outside the city.

Potential Places: Fairie Glade, Dense Woods, Scottish Moor

Palace Set

Humming with politics, the Palace is the focal point for rulers and nobles.

Potential Places: Formal Court, Extravagant Party, Solemn Coronation

Street Set

Grimy and dark, the Street is home to unwashed masses and criminals alike.

Potential Places: Den of Thieves, Open Market, Back Alley

Field Set

One of the most varied settings, the Field can be covered in blood or awash in flowers. Or both.

Potential Places: Terrible Battle, Peasant Fair, Outdoor Wedding

Church Set

Bound by rules and dogma, the Church is a beacon for those who would seek sanctuary in religion and order.

Potential Places: Private Sanctuary, Grand Cathedral, Secret Ritual

Adding Props and Places

Don't forget that you can add additional Props and Places to the stage using Edits!

As the final step in Casting the Play, The Playwright should hand out each Character's lines, a few choice selections from Shakespeare's work for each Actor. If someone is playing Hamlet, for example, The Playwright might choose:

"To be, or not to be: that is the question..."

"The lady doth protests too much me thinks."

"There are more things in heaven and earth, Horatio, than are dreamt of in your philosophy."

Each time an Actor says one of his or her lines, The Playwright should offer a story point reward. If the line is said perfectly, with much sorrow in a Tragedy or joy in a Comedy, an Actor might earn three to five story points. If the line is thrown away or totally misused, The Playwright is only obligated to give one.

Rather than have each game session sprawl over four to five game sessions, your Troupe will play out the entire play in just five scenes called Acts. Since most of Shakespeare's plays are lengthy endeavors—Kenneth Branagh's Hamlet is over four hours long!—the five Acts the Playwright selects might condense several typical scenes into a form that your Troupe can make it through quickly. (Check out the Scripts section on page 73 for a few condensed versions of Shakespeare's plays.)

Once the Actors have all been assigned Parts and Plots, the Playwright sets forward the setting of Act I. The Playwright establishes three things:

- ⟿ The *Set* and *Place* where the *Act* takes place
- ⟿ At least two *characters* who will start the Act
- ⟿ The general narrative of the Act

For example:

> "Act 1 takes place in The Palace at a Formal Court. King Lear has summoned his daughters to announce that he will step down from his throne. In this Act, Cordelia will anger him, and she will be exiled."

Keep in mind that this is not exactly how the Play will proceed. The Actors still have a chance to change the Play as it happens, perhaps saving a beloved character from an unfortunate fate or making the tragedy even more heartbreaking. The Playwright is merely laying out what the script says is going to happen. It's up to the Actors to make it more interesting...

The Whole Play

If your Troupe wants to spend multiple game sessions dealing with one Play, feel free to include Scenes within the Acts. The Playwright should give each Act a general theme and scope, but define each Scene with a separate synopsis, Set, and Characters.

Before playing the Act, the Actors must decide which Parts, Plots, and Props they will bring with them on stage. While a character may have five different Parts and five different Plots, such complexity would be beyond any actor's skill. And while an Actor may have a whole trunk of Props in her dressing room, he or she can't bring all of them on stage.

Instead, each Character element is limited by his or her Logos, Pathos, and Ethos. An Actor may only bring as many Parts as his or her Logos score, as many Plots as his or her Pathos score, and as many Props as his or her Ethos score. Any additional Parts, Plots, and Props are not brought on stage for that Act. Actors must focus on a few Parts or Plots to make sure that they are portrayed well.

If an Actor does not bring a Part or Plot to a scene, it means he or she cannot benefit from Invoking that aspect, but may still be Compelled by it. In addition, the other characters still act as if the aspect is true (i.e. people don't forget that The Ruler is the King). It is only the Invoke that doesn't count.

Adding Places

An unlimited number of Places may be added to Sets during play. The Playwright can add a new Place by spending a story point or Actors may suggest such changes as a Major Edit. Adding a Place can even happen before an Act starts, but the Actors must let The Playwright establish a Set first.

PLAYING THE ACT

Once all the pieces are in place, the Actors portray the Act "as written" as their Characters. They can narrate movements, deliver lines, and plot and plan within the limits of the narrative described by the Playwright.

For the most part, this is all free form improvisational acting. The Actors, as their Characters, take the information that the Playwright has given them as a base, and work to build a cohesive story. In each scene, they discuss and argue about the events at hand, playing their roles as if the audience was already there watching them perform.

If this all seems confusing, go check out the Replay on our website at magpiegames.com/theplayreplay. I promise it will all make sense when you see an example.

Who is talking?

To keep things clear, Players should turn their name plates around if they are stepping completely out of character, showing the rest of the game their real name to indicate who is talking. Otherwise, it should be obvious if you are speaking as your Actor instead of your Character because you should say "Cut!"

JOINING THE ACT

If a character is not onstage, they may join the Act if called by another character. For example, The Ruler may ask for his Fool, or a Lover may call out to a Knight from her open window. These summons are free. Actors can also pay three story points to the Playwright to join the scene, forcing their way onto the stage.

WOUNDED! POISONED!

During The Play, characters can be Wounded or Mortally Wounded. Wounded characters heal after one Act, but Mortally Wounded characters die at the end of the current Act. The same is true for Poisoned or Mortally Poisoned. Woundings and Poisonings are typically major plot events, and Mortal injuries are always the center of attention.

Wounding or Poisoning a character is a Minor Edit, and Mortally Wounding or Poisoning a characters is a Major Edit. The Playwright—and the Villain!—can do either by giving the targeted Character a story point.

If a Character dies in an Act, he or she gets a monologue before passing into the next world. Even if the Character has been a terrible villain, and deserves no quarter or mercy, the entire Troupe pauses to listen to the words of dying men and women.

I died!

Yup. It happens. Especially in a Tragedy. Your Playwright can cast you in a new Part when the next Act starts.

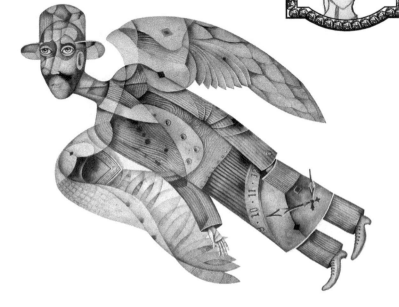

Even though the Playwright has an idea of where each Act should go—and what each Character should do—the Actors usually want to change things up. There are even times when the Actors start to make changes without realizing it! (Don't worry. Your Playwright will probably remind you that you're straying from the script.)

- *If an Actor wishes to propose a change to the Play,* he or she must spend a story point and yell "Cut!" The Actor suggests an Edit to the Playwright and the Playwright can choose to deny or accept the change.

- *If the Playwright immediately accepts the Edit,* the Playwright returns the story point spent to initiate the Cut. Usually these are ideas the Playwright hasn't thought of before, or a twist so good it can't be turned down. Well done!

- *If the Playwright rejects the Edit,* the Actor may use dice to try to Force the Edit on the Playwright. Forcing an Edit isn't a bad thing. In fact, it's kinda the point of the game. Feel free to Force Edits as much as you want!

When an Actor declares that he or she wants to Force an Edit, the Playwright should declare what type of Edit it will be. Different types of Edits have different Target Numbers that are needed for the Edit to succeed.

The Actor should gather a number of dice (as described below), and roll all of them. Then the Actor should add up his or her entire roll; if it matches or exceeds the Target Number needed, the roll Forces the Edit. If the roll is less than the Target Number, the Edit fails.

TRIVIAL, MINOR, AND MAJOR EDITS

There are three types of Edits: Trivial, Minor, and Major. Each type requires an Actor to reach a different target number to convince the Playwright that the change suggested is actually a good idea. It's easier to convince someone to change a small thing—like the color of a chair—than to change something large, like the ending of The Play.

- *Trivial Edits*: Small changes that matter only to one or two characters, such as the location of a servant or the name of a city. The Target Number for Trivial Edits is 10.
- *Minor Edits*: Moderate changes that affect the narrative, such as the Wounding of a character or a change to the Set. The Target Number for Minor Edits is 15.
- *Major Edits*: Serious changes that greatly determine the course of the Play, such as the death of a character or the addition of a Plot or Part. The Target Number for Major Edits is 20.

GATHERING DICE FOR AN EDIT

The Actor states the change he or she wants to make and gathers any dice that would be appropriate for the roll, including additional dice from Parts, Plots, and Places, narrating each addition. Plots and Parts add two dice at the cost of one story point each, and Places and Props add one die for free. The Actor can also add in Acting Chops, based on the kind of change proposed:

- *Logos Rolls*: Alteration of the events of the Play, such as reversing the outcome of a duel.
- *Pathos Rolls*: Alterations of the characters in the Play, such as adding a Plot or Part to a character.
- *Ethos Rolls*: Alterations of the setting of the Play, such as adding a detail to a room or a Prop or Place to a Set.

An Actor may only call upon only one Part, one Plot, one Place, one Prop at one time. For example:

The Earl of Kent says "I will change the King's mind so that he does not banish Cordelia (+2 Logos). It is only right that I do so, as I am his Knight (+2) and his Friend (+2). I will call upon the Formal Court, as I am making my plea formally known (+1), and I am willing to donate a bag of Coin to the kingdom as a symbol of my loyalty to the throne (+1). I get eight dice."

The Actor can also buy dice from The Playwright using story points, at the rate of one die per five story points. Usually Actors shouldn't buy more than two or three dice per roll, but The Playwright may make an exception for a particularly important Edit.

Finally, The Troupe may buy dice for a roll that one of the Actors is making by pooling story points and buying dice. These dice, however, are more expensive: buying a die for another Actor costs ten story points.

More Than One Actor

If another Actor opposes a change (or has a different idea), he or she also gathers dice in a similar manner and rolls at the same time. The highest successful roll determines the outcome of the Edit. If Actors are rolling against each other, the Troupe cannot purchase any dice, but the individual Actors who are rolling can.

RESOLVING AN EDIT

After the Edit has been resolved, the Playwright narrates how the change will take place (or not take place) depending on the outcome of the Edit. While the Edit is a great time for discussion among Actors—no one is Onstage when Actors are trying to make Edits—The Playwright should get everyone back to their Characters by saying "Action!"

When the Troupe gets to the fifth Act, the Playwright should describe not only the setting and action of the Act, but also the Ending of The Play. Each type of Play (History, Comedy, Tragedy) has a different set of ending conditions, and no matter what has happened earlier in the Troupe's version of the Play, the Ending should still meet the general guidelines.

For example, a Troupe might have already killed off Viola during the third Act of their version of *Twelfth Night*, but there still needs to be a marriage between two characters to fulfill the guidelines for Comedy. Even if that marriage seems silly or improbable, it's up to The Playwright to work it into the script and keep The Play from failing.

Once the ending comes to pass, the play is over, regardless of what other business has yet to be resolved. While there may be some plot threads that are never fully resolved, Shakespeare's plays often ended in circumstances that left audience members wondering about the eventual fates of some of their favorite characters.

Changing the end of the Play is a Major Edit, and should not be undertaken lightly…but I imagine you already knew that.

THE PLAYWRIGHT

If you've ever played roleplaying games before, you've probably figured out by this point that being the Playwright is a lot different from the usual roles of Gamemaster, Dungeon Master, or Storyteller. There is no combat or mystery in *The Play's The Thing*, no dragons for your players to defeat or vast vampiric conspiracies to uncover. In fact, you start off every session by telling your Actors exactly what's going to happen in the Play they are about to put on!

And if you haven't played roleplaying games before, I'm sure that being an Actor seems much more attractive than being a Playwright. The Playwright has to hand out story points, play the roles no one else wants to play, and keep track of what should actually be happening in The Play. It sounds much easier to just jump in as an Actor!

So why is this fun? Why would you want to be The Playwright?

For some people, there is no good answer to that question. The idea of running the show simply doesn't appeal to them. But since you're reading this section of the book, my guess is that you think being The Playwright might just be appealing…so I'll tell you why I like sitting in the director's chair.

I like being The Playwright because it lets me pick a Play that my Actors will love…and watching them rip it apart.

I like being The Playwright because I can help my Actors learn to force edits…and I see their excitement when they succeed.

I like being The Playwright because I have the toughest job in the group…spinning the story into something meaningful.

There's no one right way to be The Playwright though. In a lot of ways, you'll have to figure out for yourself what works for your Troupe, and for you personally. But in a lot of ways, The Playwright in *The Play's The Thing* has an easier job than most Gamemasters. You've got one job:

get the Actors to stick to the script… or tell them to roll the dice in order to make meaningful changes.

In the next few pages, I'm going to share some tips and tricks for making sure your Troupe has a good time playing *The Play's The Thing*. I've also included a quick summary of the different types of Plays (Comedy, Tragedy, and History) so that you have a better grasp of the setting and a Frequently Asked Questions page that should answer any inquiries you've got. There aren't any huge secrets here, but hopefully you can use these tools to help your gaming group have an awesome time every time you sit down to play the game.

Break a leg!

BE PREPARED FOR YOUR PLAY

Don't skimp on the preparation for your gaming session. Make sure you have the cast list ready to go, lines selected for each role, and the Act summaries completed before you show up to start playing. The players are obviously going to Add Parts and Plots and make Edits to the story, but you need to give them a solid base to build on.

DON'T PLAN TOO MUCH

It's tempting to try to pick a Play that's perfect for your gaming group and make your players fit the Play. For instance, you might think that the outspoken clown in your group will be the perfect Falstaff, or that a cunning and clever female player might really like to play Lady Macbeth. But don't get in the way of what your players want. Let them pick the roles for themselves, and don't be surprised when they pick a role or part you didn't expect them to pick. Part of the fun of the game is watching your players remix traditional roles into something new and different.

ENCOURAGE YOUR PLAYERS TO MAKE EDITS

I simply cannot emphasize this point enough: encourage your players to make Edits! *The Play's The Thing* isn't fun if you try to discourage your players from trying to change the plot you lay out; your players won't get involved and the game will be a huge drag. Give out story points when they suggest changes, reward them for including their lines, and always ask "Would you like to make an Edit?" They need the encouragement to learn how the game works!

Use Direction and Compels to Involve the Players

In addition to encouraging your players to make Edits, you should also get your players involved by using Direction and their Compels. Generally, I try to use one Direction per Act, and target Compels as often as I can to motivate the Characters and get story points to the Actors. The Actors can't turn down a Direction, so use it wisely and reward them with story points if they make it work well in the Act.

Focus on the Ending to Keep Things Moving

The endings of Shakespearean Plays are big, notable events. We know that Comedies end with marriages, Tragedies end in death, and Histories end with a new king (or queen). As your group makes Edits and introduces new Plots and Parts, try to steer the story back toward that ending. For example, if your tragic hero decides to play against his flaws to avoid his fate, twist that decision back on him when you announce the next Act. (See the Replay on our website for a great example of this.)

Generally speaking, Comedies focus on the courtship and romantic entanglements between two young, highborn characters. Usually there is some obstacle to the relationships, but the barrier isn't that serious. Perhaps the two characters don't have enough money to get married, or they fight too much to ever settle down with each other. This is in stark contrast to the Tragedies where the difficulties are so serious that they end in death.

Comedies also have multiple intertwining plots, and usually feature a subplot focusing on the slapstick of low-born characters. Sometimes these plots play out in parallel scenes to the main plot, but for the most part they are highly integrated. The silly, over-the-top antics of the comic relief end up charging through the slightly more serious relationships of the highborn characters all the time.

These type of plays almost always end in marriage, but they don't always tie up totally neatly—in the case of Measure for Measure, the marriage is troubling because Isabella is a novice nun; in Love Labour's Lost, the marriages are thwarted by the death of a character's father;

and in Two Gentleman of Verona, the double-marriage and redeemed friendship is, perhaps, forced. Marriages reaffirm the sanctity of the social order, but Shakespeare couldn't resist throwing in some ideas that make the audience question the social order itself.

In short:

- ↜ Romance Plots
- ↜ Young, noble characters
- ↜ Lowborn comedic characters
- ↜ End in marriage

Tips for Comedy

Your Actors should have no trouble playing out the romantic and slapstick elements of the game; most of the time, Actors love to chew the scenery with lewd jokes and silly outcomes. Make sure to give out lots of story points for funny one-liners and ironic pratfalls. Your Actors—especially those playing the low-born characters—will appreciate the encouragement!

When it comes to marriage, the Actors will usually try to rearrange things by canceling the wedding or getting married to someone completely different. This is totally fine! It's better than fine! It's perfect! Your Actors should be making changes to the play, and swapping out Characters in a marriage or changing the ending of The Play is exactly what the game is about. These are Major edits, but with the right number of dice, your Actors should be able to pull it off.

If your Actors make changes early, though, make sure to tilt the game back toward marriage and jovial jokes. It's your job as the Playwright to keep The Play from going totally off the rails. Maybe the parents of the Characters demand the wedding, or a new, lighthearted Character shows up to lighten the mood when it's getting too serious. Either way, use the rules of a Comedy as a guiding star.

Tragedies feature a hero of noble birth whose flaws lead to his or her downfall (usually, death). The machinations of fate, sometimes directly portrayed on stage by supernatural creatures like the Witches in Macbeth or Hamlet's Father's Ghost in Hamlet, push the hero toward choices that end in sadness and death for everyone involved. These choices are the crux of the play; the tragedy arises because of the hero's actions, not in spite of his best efforts.

Tragedies have fewer comedic characters and moments—although it can be easily argued that Romeo and Juliet is Shakespeare's dirtiest play up to Act 3—and tend to be deliberate and focused in their pacing. In Othello, almost all of the scenes are centered around Iago's desire to destroy the Moorish general; in Macbeth, nearly every conversation is about Macbeth's bloody quest for the Scottish throne.

These plays end with a body count, usually onstage. It's rare that the majority of the cast survives, but almost certain that the tragic hero will die. That's not to say that villains don't get what's coming to them. Most of the time the villains of the play are killed even before the hero's fate is fully revealed. Yet, the most heartbreaking moments are often when the innocent suffer for the crimes of others. Cordelia's death at the end of King Lear is so tragic that many troupes refused to play it as written for most of the 18th century.

In short:

- ❧ Flawed Hero
- ❧ Usually a single plot thrust
- ❧ End in death, usually several, mostly onstage

Tips for Tragedy

To be honest, Tragedies can be a bit of a bummer. Actors love playing these Plays because the stories are really well known, but it's not unusual for the Actors to get a bit frustrated and sad halfway through the game session. It's hard to watch a group of Characters destroy themselves, and if the Actors can't think of interesting ways to change the story, it can be a bit exhausting.

The potential for frustration means that it is really important for the Playwright to encourage the Troupe to make changes. The singular plot thrust usually found in Tragedies occasionally makes players feel like any changes will ruin the play, and it's the Playwright's job to make sure that the Troupe knows that Edits are awesome and fun. You can do this primarily by accepting changes early without making the players roll, perhaps even offering story points for good ideas.

Despite changes, it's not hard to move Tragedies toward death and destruction; the stakes—kingdoms, birthrights, true love—are pretty high in most cases, and the Characters in these plays are just dying to kill each other off. It won't take much effort to arrange for death scenes for all when your Actors get to the end of the play, and I've found that very few Actors try to avoid their fates when a Tragedy comes to a close. After all, everyone gets a monologue when they die.

Based on historical English monarchs, Histories dramatize important moments in a particular monarch's time on the throne. The entire string of plays, ranging from King John to Henry VIII, documents the rise and fall of many kings, but takes great pains to show the House of Tudor—whose Queen sat on the throne in Shakespeare's day—in a flattering light.

Due to the contentious and violent nature of conflicts between royals, these plays are often violent and grim, showcasing how one family came to control the English crown. Sometimes the monarch is portrayed as a noble hero, leading his people to victory over insurmountable odds—as in Henry V—and sometimes the monarch is shown to be a horrific monster—as in Richard III—capable of committing any atrocity in the pursuit of the crown.

Like Tragedies, Histories usually have a single plot thrust and often involve onstage battles. Most of these battles are preceded by speeches by kings and generals to motivate troops as they march forward to war. These speeches are some of the most famous passages in Shakespeare's plays, exemplifying the ability of language to inspire greatness in men.

In short:

- ↬ A dramatization of the titular monarch's reign
- ↬ Often involve onstage battles/warfare
- ↬ Often involve the overthrow of one monarch/house and the installation of a new one
- ↬ Lots of great, nationalistic speechifying

TIPS FOR HISTORY

Unlike the other types of Shakespearean Plays, Histories have a much more fluid structure from beginning to end. While the focus needs to be on the character named in the title—Richard better have a large role in Richard III—there is a lot of room to determine that character's fate and to involve new characters who plot and scheme to take the crown. To that end, your players should have a lot of leeway to add Parts or Plots and make Edits to the story, and you should encourage them to do so as much as you can.

At the same time, you should try to redirect the Troupe back toward issues of monarchy and rulership if they get off course. As interesting as Falstaff is in Henry IV, his importance is truly based on what he means to young Prince Hal's life and future kingship. Everything about the plays should reflect back onto the themes of rulership and the righteousness of just monarchy. Make sure that your Actors are constantly wrestling with these kinds of issues by goading them into leading rebellions, stealing crowns, and generally seeking power.

With that in mind, playing Histories is really about playing politics. As long as your Actors are encouraged to scheme, plot, and rebel to keep the "right" king on the throne for England, your History play will be an exciting romp through the history of the English monarchy.

If you play with the same group repeatedly, your Troupe can use the same Actors to put on a different Play. This can actually be a lot of fun because your Actors will get to know each other and reference previous experiences they've had together. Eventually it will feel like you're a real Troupe, with each member of the cast knowing the other members' habits and favorite roles.

To reward Troupes that stay together, you can let Actors keep the style they have earned from session to session, or allow them to change their Acting Chops to better suit their style of play. You might also award extra story points for particularly great moments that your Actors have in between Plays. It's up to you and your Troupe to figure out what makes playing the same Actors over and over again worth it.

CHANGING ACTOR TYPES

If your Troupe has played together for a while, it's likely that someone in the Troupe will want to change Actor Types. An Actor's Type is difficult to change, but not impossible. All it takes is one great performance to rewrite the Actor's reputation, and change what the audience will expect in the future.

After each play has ended—and all the Actors have taken their bows—any one the Actors can ask the Troupe to grant them a new Actor Type. It's up to the Troupe as a whole to rule on this; if the majority of the Actors feel that the performance was so perfect as to redefine the Actor's reputation, the Actor who requested the change gets his or her wish. If the request is denied—the majority of the Troupe doesn't think the Actor's Type should change—the Actor will have to give it another shot during the next performance.

Experience Points

The Play's The Thing is so rules-light that I haven't included any rules for giving Actors experience points. But if you really wanted to give out one or two experience points at the end of every session that players could spend to improve their Actors, here's what I'd let them spend it on:

 1 xp: +5 Story Points for the next Play
 5 xp: +1 Acting Chop (Logos, Pathos, Ethos)
10 xp: +1 New Offstage or Onstage ability

FREQUENTLY ASKED QUESTIONS:

How many story points should I give out?

A lot. Give out story points whenever you have an excuse to do so. Nothing slows down a game more than small stacks of story points in front of your players. They get worried that they won't have any left when they "need" them. Be generous!

Help! My players aren't really changing the story. What can I do to get them involved?

I think the best way to get players involved is to watch their faces closely... and suggest that they make changes when you think they want to make them. New players—and experienced players—sometimes are uncomfortable with making changes to the story, but their expressions will tell you when they don't like something or have an idea for an addition to the narrative. When you see a flicker of engagement cross their faces, jump in and ask them "Do you want to make a change?" or "Do you want to call a cut?" Eventually your players will get used to the system and start making changes without your prompting.

Help! My players murdered Macbeth in the first Act. What do I do now?

First, don't panic. I know it seems scary to have your Actors "ruin" the whole plot in the first Act, but that's kinda the point of the whole game. We want our players to mess up the story, to rearrange things so that we end up with a new version of Shakespeare's famous plays. In fact, you should probably give your whole group a bunch of story points for being so brave and ingenious!

As for actually dealing with a major Character's death early in The Play, you can try a few things:

- ↪ Ask your players what they think should happen
  - ↪ If one of them kills off Macbeth, it's likely he or she has a plan. Let them carry it out! And reward them with story points!
- ↪ Focus on the Characters that are left
  - ↪ Whoever killed Macbeth probably wants the crown for him- or herself. Is it possible that the Characters who did the killing will continue the Scottish lord's bloody plan? Is Lady Macbeth, for instance, ready to be the star of the show?
- ↪ Bring back dead Characters
  - ↪ Ghosts and the undead have a strong place in the Shakespearean canon. If you have an important dead Character on your hands, maybe he needs to come back from the dead just long enough to get the other Characters moving in the direction the play was originally moving. I can imagine that Lady Macbeth would appreciate some ghostly help from her dead husband.

How do I write a script for my favorite Shakespearean play?
We tried to include the most popular Shakespearean plays in the Scripts section of this book (see page 73), but I'm sure we missed a few of your favorite works. If you'd like to write your own Scripts, we have instructions on how to do so in that section.

When do I use Logos / Pathos / Ethos?

If the Edit affects the outcome of events, use Logos. If the Edit affects the actions of other characters, use Pathos. If the Edit affects the setting, use Ethos. Obviously there is some overlap, so feel free to use your judgement on what is most appropriate.

Can more than one character have the same Part or Plot?

Yes! In fact, it's pretty common. In a History, there will be a few Rulers and Knights; in a Tragedy, there are probably multiple In Love plots. Don't worry at all about doubling up.

SCRIPTS

Getting everything ready to play *The Play's The Thing* is sometimes more difficult than it seems. While we all think we know how Hamlet went down, it gets a bit tough to put the events in the right order and with the right characters. It's even tougher when you've got to summarize everything into just five quick Acts!

To help you out, I've provided everything you need to play through a few of Shakespeare's most famous plays: Taming of the Shrew, Macbeth, Hamlet, Richard III, and others. Each Script comes with a short synopsis of the play for your players, a Cast List with Starting Plots, Parts, and Props, lines for each Actor, and the Act summaries. In short, it's everything you need to sit down and play using a Shakespearean work you've never read.

You'll have to forgive me a bit for how much I've butchered these amazing works of art. I had to hack at the plays a bit to get them to fit the format so that your Troupe can use them. If I missed your favorite character or a perfect line, please feel free to add it back in! After all, your Actors are going to be adding their own spin as soon as you start playing.

MAKING YOUR OWN SCRIPTS

If you want to write a script for your favorite Shakespearean play, just follow these steps:

- Condense the play into five short Acts. This can be tough, but if you're willing to mutilate the work a bit, you can get it all to fit in just five major scenes. I recommend Sparknotes.com for help figuring out which scenes are important to the overall plot.
- List the Sets and Places for each Act.
- List the Characters that are important to those major scenes. Give them starting Plots, Parts, and Props.
- Find two or three great quotes for each Character. Often, you can Google search quotes based on the character's name if you're stuck. It's frustrating when you find quotes that give the Act and Scene, but not the Character, so make sure to have a copy of the actual play with you when you're doing this step.

Once you're done, send it over to us at scripts@magpiegames.com . We'd love to see it!

The Taming of the Shrew is one of Shakespeare's best known Comedies, a mix of disguised suitors and quick witted women. The maiden Bianca cannot be married until her sister, Katherine—who resists marriage by driving away men with her insults and attacks—is married. Katherine eventually finds in Petruchio a man who is her intellectual equal, but his efforts to "tame" her leave the audience wondering if they can possibly work as man and wife.

THE CAST

Bianca, the younger sister of Katherine, and daughter of Baptista

- *Starting Part/Plot/Prop:* The Maiden, Daughter to Baptista, Letter
- "I'll not be tied to hours nor appointed times, but learn my lessons as I please myself."
- "Fie! What a foolish duty call you this?"

Lucentio, a young man from Pisa who wishes to win Bianca's hand

- *Starting Part/Plot/Prop:* The Commoner, In Love with Bianca, Disguise
- "I burn, I pine, I perish, if I achieve not this young modest girl."
- "Counsel me, for I know thou canst; asset me, for I know thou will."

Baptista Minola, a rich lord of Padua whose daughters are a constant thorn in his side

- *Starting Part/Plot/Prop:* The Ruler, Father to Katherine and Bianca, Coin
- "By this reckoning he is more shrew than she."
- "Katherine the curst! A title for a maid of all titles the worst."

Katherine, the "shrew" of the title who castigates and insults men she finds disrespectful and rude

- ↝ *Starting Part/Plot/Prop:* The Maiden, Daughter to Baptista, Knife
- ↝ "If I be waspish, best beware my sting."
- ↝ "Of all things living, a man's the worst!"
- ↝ "Asses are made to bear, and so are you!"

Hortensio, a gentleman of Verona who seeks Bianca's hand in marriage.

- ↝ *Starting Part/Plot/Prop:* The Knight, Friend to Petruchio, Disguise

- ↝ "Why, so this gallant will command the sun."
- ↝ "You must, as we do, gratify this gentleman, to whom we all rest generally beholding."

Petruchio, a brash lad from Verona who seeks a rich bride to alleviate his financial troubles

- ↝ *Starting Part/Plot/Prop:* The Knight, Friend to Hortensio, Sword
- ↝ "Why, there's a wench! Come on and kiss me, Kate."
- ↝ "Women are made to bear, as so are you!"
- ↝ "Will you, nill you, I will marry you."

Act 1: Street Set—Open Market

A Lord of Padua, Baptista, proclaims that no one shall be allowed to marry Bianca until her older sister, Katherine, is married. Bianca's suitor, Hortensio is devastated; Katherine is a nasty, angry woman that no one wants to marry. Luckily for Hortensio, his friend Petruchio is looking for a wife, and Hortensio convinces him to marry Katherine. At the same time, Lucentio - a young man who falls in love with Bianca at first sight - also has plans in the works. He disguises himself as a Latin tutor to get close to Bianca and court her in private.

Act 2: Palace Set—Family Quarters

Petruchio travels to Baptista's house to ask for Katherine's hand in marriage, offering a disguised Hortensio as a music tutor for the girls. Along with the disguised Lucentio, the two girls are tutored, but things go poorly when Katherine breaks a lute over Hortensio's head. Pertruchio confronts Katherine and insists that they marry. After some disagreement,

Pertruchio tells Baptista that "Kate" has agreed to marry him… a claim she quietly accepts.

Act 3: Palace Set—Private Quarters

Just before Kate's wedding, Bianca's two suitors work to earn her attention, fighting over who should tutor her more often. Bianca eventually confesses that she prefers Latin, and Lucentio is able to relay his feelings toward her when they are alone. Kate and Petruchio are married, and Petruchio drags Kate off to his country house without giving her family time to celebrate.

Act 4: Palace Set—Country House

Petruchio attempts to "tame" Kate by refusing to let her sleep or eat, insisting that the bed and food are not good enough for his beautiful wife. Meanwhile, Bianca and Lucentio began plans to elope, knowing that Baptista will not permit her to marry the relatively poor Lucentio when other, richer suitors court Bianca. They are caught by Baptista, however, before they can elope.

Act 5: Church Set—Wedding Banquet

Petruchio and Katherine return from their country estate to find that Baptista has accepted Bianca's wishes and has allowed her to marry Lucentio, and that Hortensio has married a rich widow. The wives leave to talk, and Lucentio and Hortensio begin to chide Petruchio for marrying "a shrew." He proposes a wager: they will all call for their wives, and the first husband whose wife obeys him will win. To their surprise, Kate is the first to respond, and gives a speech about the duties a wife owes her husband.

A Comedy focused on identity and social roles, Twelfth Night is filled with characters pretending to be something they are not. Lost in the strange land of Illyria, the young lady Viola decides to dress as a man in order to join Duke Orsino's court. As she falls in love with Orsino, he orders Viola to woo his love, Lady Olivia, on his behalf. But when Lady Olivia grows enamored with the disguised Olivia the whole court is caught up in a love triangle of mistaken identities.

 THE CAST

Duke Orsino, the ruler of Illyria

- Starting Plot/Part/Prop: The Ruler, In Love with Lady Olivia, Crown
- "If music be the food of love, play on."
- "And all is semblative a woman's part"

Lady Olivia, a maiden who mourns the death of her brother

- Starting Plot/Part/Prop: The Maiden, Friend to Uncle Toby, Coin
- "O world! How apt the poor are to be proud!"
- "Why, this is very midsummer madness."

Malvolio, head servant to Lady Olivia

- Starting Plot/Part/Prop: The Commoner, Sworn to Lady Olivia, Lantern
- "Is there no respect of place, persons, nor time in you?"
- "Some are born great, some achieve greatness, and some have greatness thrust upon 'em."

Sebastian, Viola's twin brother, thought to be lost at sea

- Starting Plot/Part/Prop: The Knight, Brother to Viola, Sword
- "What relish is in this? How runs the stream? Or I am mad, or else this is a dream."

Uncle Toby, Lady Olivia's oft-inebriated uncle	*Viola*, a young woman shipwrecked on the Illyrian coast
↦ Starting Plot/Part/Prop: The Knight, Rival to Malvolio, Sword	↦ Starting Plot/Part/Prop: The Maiden, Sister to Sebastian, Disguise
↦ "I'll confine myself no finer than I am."	↦ "Whoe'er I woo, myself would be his wife"
↦ "Dost thou think, because thou art virtuous, there shall be no more cakes and ale?"	↦ "She sat like Patience on a monument, smiling at grief."

Act 1: Palace Set—The Duke's Court

Viola is shipwrecked on the Illyrian coast, separated from her twin brother, Sebastian. Viola decides to disguise herself as a boy—Cesario—to enter Duke Orsino's service. Immediately impressed with his new manservant, Orsino sends Viola to woo Lady Olivia, insisting that Cesario's attractiveness will win Olivia over. Viola, flattered by Orsino's compliments, realizes she is in love with Duke Orsino, but goes to woo Lady Olivia on his behalf. Viola is uninterested in Orsino, but tells Cesario that he is welcome to return anytime he likes.

Act 2: Palace Set—Servant's Quarters

Uncle Toby, tired of Malvolio's constant complaining about Toby's drinking and carousing, prepares a practical joke for his niece's servant. Working with the other servants, Uncle Toby leaves a note out for Malvolio that convinces the head servant that Olivia loves him, but requires that he dress and behave in an outlandish manner to prove he loves Lady Olivia as well. Malvolio, convinced that the letter is genuine, prepares to make a fool of himself for love.

Act 3: Palace Set—Private Quarters

Viola returns to speak with Lady Olivia, still dressed as Cesario, on behalf of Duke Orsino. Olivia rejects any mention of Orsino and confesses that she loves Cesario, and wishes to marry him. Viola, in turn, rejects Lady

Olivia, and tells her that no maiden shall win her heart. Saddened by the rejection, Olivia calls for Malvolio to make her feel better, but he arrives wearing ridiculous clothing and behaving in irritating ways. As Lady Olivia storms out, Uncle Toby begins to plot further mayhem for Malvolio.

Act 4: Street Set—Open Market

Lady Olivia wanders the streets of Illyria looking for Cesario. She stumbles upon Sebastian, who survived the shipwreck, and mistakes him for Cesario. She proposes marriage, and Sebastian—immediately enamored with the beautiful noblewoman—accepts. The two are married. Meanwhile, Sir Toby has Malvolio locked up, claiming that the head servant has gone crazy.

Act 5: Palace Set—The Lady's Court

Viola (disguised as Cesario) and Duke Orsino call upon Lady Olivia. When they arrive, Olivia is confused by Cesario's continued loyalty to Duke Orsino, believing that she has already married Cesario. Cesario denies the marriage, and chaos erupts. Sir Toby and Sebastian enter, and the two siblings finally reunite. Viola reveals that she is a woman, and Duke Orsino—finally accepting that Lady Olivia does not love him—proposes to Viola, and calls upon the whole land to celebrate the double marriage. Malvolio is released from the madhouse, but swears revenge upon them all…

Set at Leonado's Estate, in the city of Messina, Much Ado About Nothing is a flurry of wit and social misunderstandings. Young Claudio attempts to woo his host Leonado's daughter with the help of his friend Don Pedro, but has his efforts are repeatedly sabotaged by Don Pedro's resentful half brother, Don John the Bastard. Meanwhile, the battle of wits between Benedick and Beatrice inspires their friends and families to conspire to get them to fall in love with each other.

 THE CAST

Don Pedro, the Prince

- Starting Plot/Part/Prop: The Ruler, Brother to Don Juan, Crown

- "I shall see thee, ere I die, look pale with love."

- "Speak low, if you speak love."

Benedick, a companion to Don Pedro and a sworn bachelor

- Starting Plot/Part/Prop: The Fool, Friend to Don Pedro, Lute

- "What, my dear Lady Disdain! are you yet living?"

- "I should think this a gull, but that the white-bearded fellow speaks it: knavery cannot, sure, hide himself in such reverence."

- "Come, bid me do any thing for thee."

- "Thou and I are too wise to woo peaceably."

Claudio, a companion to Don Pedro who falls in love with Hero

- ↪ Starting Plot/Part/Prop: The Hero, Friend to Don Pedro, Sword
- ↪ "Friendship is constant in all other things save in the office and affairs of love"
- ↪ "Your over-kindness doth wring tears from me!"

Don John, Don Pedro's illegitimate half-brother

- ↪ Starting Plot/Part/Prop: The Exile, Rival to Don Pedro, Letter
- ↪ "If I had my mouth, I would bite."

Borachio, a companion to Don John

- ↪ Starting Plot/Part/Prop: The Knight, Pawn to Don Juan, Sword
- ↪ "The poison of that lies in you to temper."
- ↪ "If you would know your wronger, look on me."

Leonado, Governor of Messina

- ↪ Starting Plot/Part/Prop: The Ruler, Father to Hero, Crown
- ↪ "O, my lord, wisdom and blood combating in so tender a body, we have ten proofs to one that blood hath the victory."
- ↪ "Being that I flow in grief, the smallest twine may lead me".
- ↪ "Bring me a father that so loved his child, whose joy of her is overwhelm'd like mine, and bid him speak of patience"

- ↪ "If thou kill'st me, boy, thou shalt kill a man."

Hero, Leonado's daughter

- ↪ Starting Plot/Part/Prop: The Maiden, Daughter to Leonado, Coin
- ↪ "I will do any modest office, my lord, to help my cousin to a good husband."
- ↪ "Is it not Hero? Who can blot that name with any just reproach?"

Beatrice, Leonado's niece, who has sworn not to marry

- ↪ Starting Plot/Part/Prop: The Maiden, Friend to Hero, Knife
- ↪ "I had rather hear my dog bark at a crow than a man swear he loves me."
- ↪ "O God, that I were a man! I would eat his heart in the marketplace."
- ↪ "Foul words is but foul wind, and foul wind is but foul breath, and foul breath is noisome; therefore I will depart unkissed."

Act 1: Palace Set—Leonardo's Estate

Don Pedro returns from battle with his brother, accompanied by his friends Benedick and Claudio, and his brother Don John. The party plans to stay at Leonado's estate. Don Pedro and Benedick note Claudio's admiration for Leonado's daughter, Hero, and Don Pedro offers to help Claudio woo her, while Benedick defends the bachelor's life. The rumor of this exchange reaches Leonado and Antonio, but they mishear the story as Don Pedro wooing Hero. Don John, who sees it as a chance to cause trouble for Claudio, who was instrumental in his defeat.

Act 2: Palace Set—Masquerade Party

Leonado throws a masquerade party. Behind a mask, Don Pedro woos Hero in the name of Claudio. Don John approaches Claudio and begs him to warn Don Pedro away from his plan to marry Hero. Don John's plan to interfere is ruined when Don Pedro proclaims that Hero has agreed to to marry Claudio. After witnessing the two argue, Don Pedro, Leonado, and Hero hatch a plan to bring Benedick and Beatrice together and arrange for Benedick to eavesdrop on a conversation about how Beatrice is in love with him. Benedick decides to return her "affection."

Act 3: Palace Set—Private Quarters

Hero tells Beatrice that Benedick is sick with love for her, and Beatrice decides that if he loves her that much, she can return his love. Don John has his companion Borachio seduce a servant and call her "Hero" within the hearing of Don Pedro and Claudio to stir Claudio's jealousy.

Act 4: Church Set—Royal Wedding

At their wedding the next day, Claudio declares that Hero has been with other men, shocking everyone. After Claudio and Don Pedro leave, Beatrice declares that she has long shared a room with Hero and the accusations are false. It is suggested that they pretend that Hero has died until the truth has been proven.

Act 5: Church Set—Royal Wedding

Leonado tells Don Pedro and Claudio that Hero is dead. Benedick rejects his companions out of loyalty to Beatrice. Guilty over Hero's death, Borachio confesses to Don Pedro and Leonado. Don John flees, but is caught and arrested. Out of shame, Claudio asks how he can make up for his accusations. Leonado states that he has a relative, much like Hero, that Claudio can marry instead. At the wedding, it is revealed that this is Hero. Benedick and Beatrice are tricked into confessing their love, discover the scheme of their friends and family and decide to marry as well.

The tragic tale of Othello, a Christian Moor who has arisen to the rank of general in Venice, is testament to the wicked temptations of jealousy. Driven by ambition, Othello's foil Iago uses all his powers of persuasion to turn Othello against his new bride Desdemona, arranging for Othello to murder her in a jealous rage. Yet, Iago cannot escape the violence; the Duke of Venice sentences him to death for his treachery.

 THE CAST

Cassio, the loyal lieutenant of Othello, recently promoted ahead of Iago.

- ✎ *Starting Part/Plot/Prop:* The Knight, Sworn to Othello, Sword
- ✎ "Reputation, reputation, reputation! Oh, I have lost my reputation! I have lost the immortal part of myself, and what remains is bestial."
- ✎ "I have very poor and unhappy brains for drinking."

Desdemona, Othello's new wife, a daughter of a Venetian Senator.

- ✎ *Starting Part/Plot/Prop:* The Maiden, In Love with Othello, Letter
- ✎ "I do perceive here a divided duty."
- ✎ "Heaven me such uses send, Not to pick bad from bad, but by bad mend."

Iago, the jealous ensign of Othello's army, a cold man who is obsessive in his desire to see Othello destroyed.

- ✎ *Starting Part/Plot/Prop:* The Commoner, Betrayer of Othello, Knife
- ✎ "Your daughter and the Moor are now making the beast with two backs."
- ✎ "O, beware, my lord, of jealousy! It is the green-eyed monster which doth mock the meat it feeds on."

Othello, a Christian Moor, an outsider to Venice who has nevertheless earned the respect of The Duke and Senate.

⮞ *Starting Part/Plot/Prop:* The Ruler, In Love with Desdemona, Sword

⮞ "Keep up your bright swords, for the dew will rust them."

⮞ "Put out the light, and then put out the light."

Act 1: Palace Set—The Duke's Court

Iago has started a rumor that Othello won over Desdemona through witchcraft. Called before the Duke of Venice, Othello explains that he won Desdemona through his stories of adventure and war. Desdemona confirms this, and insists that she loves Othello. The Duke is moved by their words, and proclaims that their love is true.

Act 2: Street Set—A Drunkard's Bar

Iago gets Cassio drunk and convinces him to start a fight with a rival officer. Cassio wounds the officer, and Othello is summoned to deal with the fighting caused by his men. Iago "reluctantly" tells Othello that it was Cassio that started the fight, and Othello strips Cassio of his title. When Othello leaves, Iago tells Cassio that he should attempt to win over Othello by pleading directly to Desdemona.

Act 3: Palace Set—Desdemona's Chambers

Cassio appeals to Desdemona to help him earn Othello's forgiveness, a cause to which she is sympathetic. Cassio leaves before Othello returns, however, and Iago uses this to convince Othello that Desdemona has betrayed him with Cassio. Desedemona makes things worse by attempting to convince Othello to forgive Cassio, arousing Othello's suspicions. Iago steals Desdemona's handkerchief and plants it on Cassio.

Act 4: Palace Set—Othello's Chambers

Othello—growing more suspicious of Desdemona—asks Iago for evidence. Iago suggests that he has seen Cassio with Desdemona's handkerchief. Othello asks Desdemona for her handkerchief, which she confesses that she has lost, and attempts to change the subject by pleading Cassio's case. Othello is enraged.

Act 5: Palace Set—Desdemona's Chambers

Othello confronts Desdemona about her relationship with Cassio, but does not believe her defense. He kills her. After her death, he realizes what has happened and confronts Iago. They duel and both are wounded. The Duke, called by servants upon the murder of Desdemona, orders that Othello be taken to Venice for trial and Iago be executed. Othello kills himself with a hidden sword before he can be taken away.

Set in dank castles and stormy moors, Macbeth's dark tone is a perfect backdrop for a tale of power-hungry murderers who conspire to steal the Scottish crown. Spurred on by supernatural prophecies, Macbeth and his wife, Lady Macbeth, carve a bloody path through Scotland, killing friends and enemies alike. Yet, their rule is short-lived. Macduff, a fellow Scottish noble, kills Macbeth on the battlefield to restore the rightful heir to the throne, Malcolm.

⟋⟍ THE CAST ⟋⟍

Banquo, a noble Scottish General, sworn to serve King Duncan

- ⤷ *Starting Part/Plot/Prop:* The Knight, Friend to Macbeth, Sword
- ⤷ "What, can the devil speak true?"
- ⤷ "Thou hast it now, as the weird women promised, and I fear thou play'dst most foully for it."

Lady Macbeth, Macbeth's fearsome wife, a sharp-tongued, aggressive woman who lusts for power

- ⤷ *Starting Part/Plot/Prop:* The Maiden, Sworn to Macbeth, Knife
- ⤷ "I fear thy nature; it is too full o' the milk of human kindness."
- ⤷ "Screw your courage to the sticking-place."
- ⤷ "When our actions do not, our fears do make us traitors."
- ⤷ "Out, damned spot! Out, I say!"

Macbeth, a Scottish General who secretly wishes to take the Scottish throne

- ⤷ *Starting Part/Plot/Prop:* The Knight, Sworn to Lady Macbeth, Sword
- ⤷ "Stars, hide your fires! Let not light see my black and deep desires."
- ⤷ "Life is a tale, told by an idiot, full of sound and fury, signifying nothing."
- ⤷ "Is this a dagger which I see before me, the handle toward my hand?"

Macduff, a Scottish nobleman who becomes suspicious of Macbeth's rise to power

- ✎ *Starting Part/Plot/Prop:* The Hero, Enemy to Macbeth, Sword
- ✎ "Dispute it as a man? I shall do so, but I must also feel it as a man."
- ✎ 'Macduff was from his mother's womb untimely ripp'd"

Malcolm, son of King Duncan

- ✎ *Starting Part/Plot/Prop:* The Hero, Rival to Macbeth, Standard
- ✎ "Angels are bright still, though the brightest fell."

- ✎ "Give sorrow words: the grief that does not speak whispers the o'er-fraught heart, and bids it break.

The Witches, the Fates whose prophecies inspire Macbeth's awful deeds

- ✎ *Starting Part/Plot/Prop:* The Witch, Betrayer of Macbeth, Poison
- ✎ "Fair is foul, and foul is fair."
- ✎ "Double, double toil and trouble; fire burn and cauldron bubble."
- ✎ "By the pricking of my thumb, something wicked this way comes."

Act 1: Field Set—Scottish Moor

Macbeth and Banquo, returning home from a great battle, come upon the Three Witches on a Scottish Moor. The Witches tell Macbeth he will be King of Scotland, but also tell Banquo that his sons will be Kings. When he arrives home and tells Lady Macbeth, Macbeth is surprised to find that she insists that he kill King Duncan and take the throne. He is hesitant, but is ultimately persuaded.

Act 2: Palace Set—Royal Quarters

Macbeth kills King Duncan, but forgets to leave the bloody dagger in the servant's quarters to frame them for the crime. Lady Macbeth covers for his error. Macduff arrives the next day, and finds King Duncan's body when he attempts to wake him. He is doubly suspicious when Macbeth reveals that he has killed the servants who murdered the King. Macduff is crowned King by the assembled lords, including Banquo. King Duncan's son, Malcolm, flees for England.

Act 3: Palace Set—Royal Feast

Macbeth, fearful that the second half of the prophecy will come true, orders Banquo murdered. The murderers kill Banquo, but fail to kill his son, Fleance. Macbeth is upset at the news, but is even more upset when Banquo's ghost starts to haunt his coronation feast. When the feast ends, Macbeth learns that Macduff has fled for England, and suspects that he will ally himself with Malcolm.

Act 4: Field Set—Scottish Moor

Macbeth returns to see The Witches, who tell him that he should fear Macduff, that "none of woman born shall harm Macbeth," and that his rule is assured until the forest moves to his castle. Macbeth is elated, but when The Witches march a line of kings in front of him, Banquo's ghost walks with the royal monarchs. Macbeth, filled with frustration, orders Macduff's family killed.

Act 5: Field Set—Terrible Battle

Macduff and Malcolm return to Scotland with an English army. In order to obscure their numbers, they cut down boughs from the forest and march on Macbeth's castle. Lady Macbeth, plagued by visions of the murders she's committed, kills herself. Macbeth, realizing that the Witches' prophecy is coming true, marches out to meet Macduff on the battlefield. Macbeth and Macduff duel, and Macduff reveals that he was "ripped" from his mother's womb instead of born. Macduff kills Macbeth and the Scottish Lords put Malcolm on the throne.

One of Shakespeare's darkest Tragedies, King Lear is the story of a king who rejects those who truly love him and favors those who flatter him with false words. Aging and tired, King Lear summons his three daughters to him to divide his kingdom among them, demanding that they prove their love with public pronouncements. When the youngest—Cordelia—refuses to speak to his liking, he banishes her, and finds himself at the mercy of his other daughters—Regan and Goneril—who do everything in their power to humiliate and destroy the former king. While Cordelia returns with a French army to free England from her sisters' tyranny, both she and her father find only death in the end.

Cordelia, the youngest daughter of King Lear

- *Starting Part/Plot/Prop:* The Maiden, Daughter to Lear, Standard

- "Unhappy that I am, I cannot heave my heart into my mouth."

- "Time shall unfold what plighted cunning hides."

Earl of Kent, loyal courtier of King Lear

- *Starting Part/Plot/Prop:* The Knight, Sworn to Lear, Sword

- "I have a journey, sir, shortly to go. My master calls me; I must not say no."

- "Vex not his ghost: O! let him pass."

The Fool, King Lear's fool

- *Starting Part/Plot/Prop:* The Fool, Friend to Lear, Lute

- "Truth's a dog must to kennel; he must be whipped out, when Lady the brach may stand by the fire and stink."

- "He's mad, that trusts in the tameness of a wolf, a horse's health, a boy's love, or a whore's oath."

Goneril, one of Lear's cruel daughters

- *Starting Part/Plot/Prop:* The Maiden, Daughter to Lear, Poison

- "Sir, I love you more than word can wield the matter, dearer than eyesight."

- "Tis his own blame hath put himself from reat, and must needs taste his folly."

King Lear, the aging King of England

- *Starting Part/Plot/Prop:* The Ruler, Father to Cordelia, Crown

- "Nothing can come of nothing: speak again."

- "Blow, winds, and crack your cheeks! Rage! Blow!"

- "I am a man, more sinn'd against than sinning."

Regan, one of Lear's cruel daughters

- *Starting Part/Plot/Prop:* The Maiden, Daughter to Lear, Letter

- "Tis the infirmity of his age: yet he hath ever but slenderly known himself."

- "Go, thrust him out at gates, and let him smell his way to Dover."

Act 1: Palace Set—Formal Court

King Lear, the ancient ruler of England, announces that he will divide his kingdom amongst his three daughters, awarding the largest share to the daughter that claims to love him most. Regan and Goneril speak at length about their love for their father, but Cordelia refuses to speak at length, plainly stating that she loves him as a daughter should love a father. He angrily banishes her from the kingdom and gives her share of the kingdom to her sisters. When the Earl of Kent attempts to persuade him otherwise, Lear banishes Kent as well. Unwilling to leave the King's side, Kent disguises himself as a common knight and joins the King's men.

Act 2: Palace Set—Royal Quarters

With Cordelia and Kent banished, Lear—accompanied by Kent and his Fool—spends his time at Regan and Goneril's estates. When they punish Kent for fighting with their servants, Lear is furious, demanding to know why they feel they can treat his men poorly. Regan and Goneril turn on the old man, demanding that he give up all his knights and servants in order to stay with them. Shocked and scared, Lear leaves the castle and heads out into the wilderness with The Fool, despite a brewing storm.

Act 3: Field Set—Stormy Heath

Lear and The Fool wander through the ferocious storm; Lear curses the forces of nature and rants about his cruel and evil daughters. As the storm blows and gusts, Kent finds the two of them, and—believing Lear to be mad—ushers them to safety. He relays to them that Cordelia has raised an army in France, and may be coming to rescue Lear from Regan and Goneril. Meanwhile, Regan and Goneril grow suspicious of each other, each believing that the other wishes to seize the entire kingdom.

Act 4: Field Set—French Army Camp

Lear, The Fool, and Kent arrive at the French army's encampment, but Lear refuses to see Cordelia, ashamed of the way he treated her in Act

CHAPTER 5

1. He flees back into the wilderness. Cordelia sends men after him, and consults a doctor about Lear's sanity. When her men retrieve Lear, he confesses that he fears Cordelia, knowing that she could be rightfully angry at him. Cordelia forgives him and ushers him off to sleep as she prepares to face her sisters' armies.

Act 5: Palace Set—Royal Quarters

Regan and Goneril's combined forces destroy Cordelia's French army, and both Cordelia and Lear are captured. Yet, Regan and Goneril's victory is short-lived; their reign collapses due to infighting and violence. After fatally poisoning Regan, Goneril commits suicide. While the tyranny has ended, freedom comes too late for Cordelia; she is hanged before Lear can stop the executioners. As he mourns over her corpse, he dies as well, leaving Kent to care for England.

Often regarded as Shakespeare's magnum opus, Hamlet is as rich and complex a play as can be created on stage, touching upon themes of love, death, madness, and family with humor, sadness, and depth. In the play, the young prince Hamlet returns home to Denmark to find that his father is dead and his Uncle Claudius has married his mother. Already troubled by the marriage, Hamlet's worst fears are confirmed when his father's ghost reveals that Claudius murdered Hamlet's father. Hamlet vows revenge, but his struggle to settle himself with the task before him eventually draws the entire court into his bloody feud.

 THE CAST

King Claudius, Hamlet's uncle and King of Denmark

- *Starting Part/Plot/Prop:* The Ruler, Enemy of Hamlet, Crown
- "My words fly up, my thoughts remain below: words without thoughts never to heaven go."
- "There's matter in these sighs, these profound heaves: you must translate."
- "To bear all smooth and even, this sudden sending him away must seem deliberate pause."

Queen Gertrude, Hamlet's mother and Queen of Denmark

- *Starting Part/Plot/Prop:* The Ruler, Mother of Hamlet, Crown
- "Thou know'st 'tis common; all that lives must die, passing through nature to eternity."
- "The lady doth protest too much, methinks."

Ophelia, Hamlet's former lover

- *Starting Part/Plot/Prop:* The Maiden, In Love with Hamlet, Letter
- "Take these again; for to the noble mind, rich gifts wax poor when givers prove unkind."
- "O, what a noble mind is here o'erthrown!"

Prince Hamlet, young prince of Denmark

- *Starting Part/Plot/Prop:* The Hero, Enemy to Claudius, Sword
- "A little more than kin, and less than kind."
- "I will speak daggers to her, but use none."
- "Alas, poor Yorick! I knew him, Horatio: a fellow of infinite jest, of most excellent fancy."

Horatio, a friend to Prince Hamlet

- *Starting Part/Plot/Prop:* The Knight, Friend to Hamlet, Lantern
- "And then it started like a guilty thing upon a fearful summons."
- "Now cracks a noble heart. Good night sweet prince: and flights of angels sing thee to thy rest!"

Laertes, a young student and the brother of Ophelia

- *Starting Part/Plot/Prop:* The Knight, Rival to Hamlet, Sword
- "Now pile your dust upon the quick and dead, till of this flat a mountain you have made."
- "The chariest maid is prodigal enough, if she unmask her beauty to the moon."

Polonius, a Danish lord

- *Starting Part/Plot/Prop:* The Fool, Father to Ophelia and Laertes, Letter
- "Neither a borrower nor a lender be; for loan oft loses both itself and friend, and borrowing dulls the edge of husbandry."
- "Therefore, since brevity is the soul of wit, and tediousness the limbs and outward flourishes, I will be brief."

Act 1: Palace Set—The Outer Gates

While patrolling the Outer Gates, Horatio sees Hamlet's father's ghost. He summons Hamlet, who pursues the ghost into the darkness, hoping to receive guidance. The ghost tells Hamlet that Claudius murdered him, and that Claudius stole his throne and Hamlet's mother. Hamlet, already suspicious of his uncle, vows revenge on the new King, but is obviously shaken by the ghost himself.

Act 2: Palace Set—Private Quarters

Ophelia and Polonius discuss Hamlet's increasingly erratic behavior, and Ophelia worries that he has been driven mad by love. Polonius approaches Claudius and Gertrude with a plan to observe Hamlet and Ophelia in order to discern the source of Hamlet's madness. Hamlet meets the players and is impressed with the depth of emotion they can summon. Hamlet decides to have the players mirror his father's death when performing for Claudius, watching closely for a sign of guilt on his uncle's face.

Act 3 (Part 1): Palace Set—The Halls of Power

Ophelia and Hamlet meet while Claudius and Polonius observe from hiding. Hamlet is cruel to Ophelia, insisting that he does not love her and that women are liars and thieves. Afterward, Claudius and Polonius agree that Hamlet's madness is not caused by love, and begin to worry about Hamlet's plans. At the play, Claudius reacts as Hamlet expects, fleeing from the room when Hamlet's father's death is reenacted.

Act 3 (Part 2): Palace Set—Private Quarters

Hamlet gives chase, and finds his uncle in prayer in the chapel. Fearing that murdering his uncle in mid-prayer would send him to heaven, Hamlet leaves Claudius unharmed and goes to see Queen Gertrude. Polonius, who knows that Hamlet is angry and potentially dangerous, hides in Queen Gertrude's room behind a curtain. When Hamlet arrives, he immediately begins to verbally attack the Queen for marrying his uncle. Hamlet hears a noise from the curtain, and—believing him to be Claudius—murders Polonius.

Act 4: Palace Set—The King's Quarters

Laertes arrives in Denmark, furious with Hamlet and ready to seek his revenge. Claudius delays him, convincing the young student to draw Hamlet into a formal duel where Laertes can use a poisoned sword. Laertes agrees to the plan, and Claudius—hedging his bet—also plans to poison a victory drink for Hamlet in case his nephew wins the duel. Meanwhile, Ophelia, driven mad by the death of her father and the loss of her love, commits suicide by drowning herself in the river.

Act 5: Palace Set—Formal Duel

Hamlet interrupts Ophelia's funeral, claiming that he loved her above all others. Laertes is eager to avenge himself, but Claudius holds him back, reminding him of their plan. Claudius proposes a duel, and both young men agree. During the duel, Hamlet gets the better of Laertes, but Laertes manages to score a hit with the poisoned weapon. The duel devolves into a brawl, and the two men exchange swords; Hamlet wounds Laertes with the poisoned sword. Gertrude, unaware of the plot, drinks from the poisoned cup. Laertes exposes Claudius, and Hamlet murders the King. Hamlet and Laertes exchange forgiveness, and they both die, leaving only Horatio to tell Hamlet's story.

Verging on a Tragedy, the tale of Richard III confirms that even the hint of absolute power corrupts. Willing to murder his wife, his brothers, and even his nephews and nieces, Richard violates the whole of England in his quest for the crown. Eventually the Earl of Richmond, a noble who rallies men to him to defeat the evil Richard on the battlefield, brings him low. Richard dies at Richmond's hand, and Richmond is crowned king after the battle.

THE CAST

Clarence, Richard's older brother and his first familial victim

- *Starting Part/Plot/Prop:* The Exile, Brother to Richard, Lute
- "I will send you to my brother Richard, who shall reward you better for my life."
- "Richard loves me, and he holds me dear."

King Edward IV, Clarence and Richard's older brother who sits on the throne of England

- *Starting Part/Plot/Prop:* The Ruler, Brother to Richard, Crown
- "Who spoke of brotherhood? Who spoke of love?"
- "At peace my soul shall part to the heavens since I have made my friends at peace on earth."

Lady Anne, widow of Henry VI's son Edward and the target of Richard's lust

- ↬ *Starting Part/Plot/Prop:* The Maiden, Enemy to Richard, Knife
- ↬ "No beast so fierce but knows some touch of pity."
- ↬ "O wonderful, when devils tell the truth."

Prince Edward, the eldest of King Edward's sons who sees through Richard's treachery

- ↬ *Starting Part/Plot/Prop:* The Hero, Son of Elizabeth, Coin
- ↬ "I fear no uncles dead."

Queen Elizabeth, Edward's wife and protector of his two young children

- ↬ *Starting Part/Plot/Prop:* The Ruler, In Love with Edward, Crown
- ↬ "If he were dead, what would become of me?"
- ↬ "Shall I be tempted by the devil then?"

Richard III, a murderous and effective liar whose physical deformities echo his awful soul

- ↬ Starting Part/Plot/Prop: The Knight, Betrayer of Edward, Sword
- ↬ "Was ever woman in this humor wooed? Was ever woman in this humor won?"
- ↬ "A horse! A horse! My kingdom for a horse!"
- ↬ "Conscience is a word that cowards use."

Earl of Richmond, a noble of strong heart who rises to oppose Richard's murderous reign

- ↬ *Starting Part/Plot/Prop:* The Hero, Enemy to Richard, Sword
- ↬ "In the name of God and all these rights, advance your standards, draw your willing swords."
- ↬ "Proclaim a pardon for the soldiers fled."

Act 1: Palace Set—Corridors of Power

Richard III has made King Edward suspicious of Clarence, resulting in Clarence's imprisonment in the Tower of England. Richard goes to visit Clarence before he is imprisoned, and claims that he will work hard to secure Clarence's release. Later, Richard confronts Lady Anne at her husband's funeral and attempts to woo her. She resists (Richard killed her husband!), but he is so charming that she begins to succumb to his words. Richard celebrates by sending hired thugs to kill Clarence in the Tower.

Act 2: Palace Set—Formal Court

King Edward summons all of the characters to him in order to make peace amongst the warring factions of his realm. He offers to rescind Clarence's death sentence, but Richard reveals it is already too late; Clarence is dead. Edward is devastated by the news, and exits the stage. His wife, Elizabeth, enters a few minutes later to tell the assembly that the King has died. Fearing for her life, Elizabeth flees with her youngest son to seek sanctuary from Richard.

Act 3: Palace Set—Noble Council

Prince Edward arrives in London; Richard has him and his brother placed in the Tower of London, claiming it will protect them. Richard calls a council, claiming to determine when Prince Edward will be crowned king, but instead uses the meeting to determine which of the nobles will support him. Richard sentences those who speak out against him to death. The mayor of London, at Richard's urging, begs Richard to take the crown to protect England. Richard "reluctantly" takes the throne and marries Lady Anne.

Act 4: Palace Set—Private Quarters

Richard orders the deaths of the two princes and his wife, Lady Anne. He attempts to convince Elizabeth to allow him to marry her daughter—and his niece—young Elizabeth. Elizabeth is reluctant; she has promised young Elizabeth to the earl of Richmond, a noble who is raising an army to invade England and kill Richard. She promises Richard that she will consider his proposal. Richard is notified that Richmond is amassing an army and leaves to crush the rebellion.

Act 5: Field Set—Terrible Battle

Richard prepares for battle, but in his sleep is haunted by ghosts. Each of his victims stands before him, condemning him to death and cursing him. Those same victims tell Richmond, in parallel, that he will be victorious on the battlefield. When the two meet on the field, Richmond kills Richard, and offers a pardon to all of Richard's men. Richmond is crowned king and married young Elizabeth to restore the noble line.

CHAPTER 5

ROMANCE & RESOURCES

Romances (or tragicomedies) are Shakespeare's late plays, a small collection of works that reflect Shakespeare's growing sense of his legacy as a playwright. Complicated tales of past wrongs and present reconciliations, the Romance plays often function as two-part or three-part stories, telling a tale of before and after that is centered around the actions of a powerful, insightful figure such as Prospero from The Tempest or Paulina in A Winter's Tale. Yet, as emotionally complex as these Plays can be, they are fairytale like in their delivery, centering around archetypal characters that embody large ideals of rulership, heroism, and courtly love.

The Romances also include supernatural elements, music, and themes of exploration, especially the discovery of new areas of the world. Oftentimes this makes Romances some of the most exciting and revelatory plays, as Shakespeare pushed the boundaries of what was possible on the Elizabethan stage by including exotic locales and fantastic interactions. A good deal of the stage direction is lively and intriguing, culminating in one of the most famous Shakespearean stage directions: Exit, pursued by bear.

Like Comedies, most Romances end in marriage, but the context is markedly different. Rather than celebrating the existing social order through the bonds of matrimony, the marriage at the end of a Romance reunites two communities or individuals who were driven apart in the past, healing the social fabric that had previously been torn asunder. The marriage affirms the social order, but simultaneously reveals the fragility of the society in which it takes place.

In short:

- ↦ Magical, fairy tale like stories
- ↦ Focused on the journey from before to after
- ↦ Iconic characters (hero, princess, magician)
- ↦ Lots of music

New Rules for Romance

Reduce the Target Numbers

Romances are tragicomic journeys through magical settings, challenging the characters' identities and, on some occasions, sanity. The stories are looser, less formulaic, and a bit wacky, which should mean more Edits from the Actors. Lower the Target Number of all Edits by five making Trivial, Minor, and Major Edits only 5, 10, and 15 respectively.

Call for Flashbacks

Since Romances occur over lengthy periods of time—sometimes stretching over decades—the Actors can challenge the linear narrative a bit by introducing Flashbacks, detours in the narrative that explain how the current situation came to be. In order to introduce a Flashback, an Actor must spend 5 story points and make a Major Edit. If the Actor is successful, the entire Troupe turns the clock back to a scene that occurred in the past, either playing their current parts, or getting new parts from The Playwright that fit the scene. Once the Flashback is finished, the story returns to the scene that was interrupted.

Introduce Magic

While some Plays have magical creatures like Faeries, Romances have items and spells that make magic available to everyone. Prospero's staff, for example, allows him to call forth a mighty storm and control Ariel and Caliban, and other Characters could make use of that same power. While Edits technically make anything possible, these kinds of magic items allow Characters to bring people back from the dead, manipulate the natural world, and perform amazing feats.

"I spent a lot of time on my own working out the physical vocabulary for how Gollum moved. [...] I'd go off and just get into character by crawling around these rocky streams on my own for hours and hours, just trying to sense that isolation really."
—Andy Serkis

Famous Examples: Charlie Chaplin, Djimon Hounsou, Doug Jones

The Mask sees acting differently than the rest of the Troupe. While they obsess over the delivery of a line, or the timing of a smile, The Mask knows that his face is only a small fraction of his instrument. It is the body he wishes to perfect, his entire form becomes his emotive weapon.

Thus, The Mask's strength lies in his physicality, the way his body makes his presence on the stage larger, more captivating. Perhaps he leaps and tumbles across the stage, or merely glides elegantly across the floor. Either way, he stands out, even when wrapped in a full-body costume or covered in costume pieces. He can move an audience without opening his mouth.

On occasion, such actors feel underused and undervalued. They are infinitely talented, but the audience can mistake their gifts for a parlor trick, a circus sideshow amongst the more legitimate thespians. Make no mistake about it; The Mask works hard at his craft, and his roles show the effort he expends in every calculated gesture.

- *Onstage Ability:* The Mask knows how unnerve anyone, even his fellow actors. You may spend a story point to make another Actor reroll a successful Edit.
- *Offstage Ability:* The Mask is always watching, always listening to the plots of others. Spend a story point to overhear a secret from the shadows.
- *Direction:* At the Playwright's request, the Mask must tell his story by describing his actions.

THE MAGICIAN

You have studied forgotten magic. You are not to be trusted.

- ↜ *Invoke:* Gain two dice when utilizing your occult skills.
- ↜ *Compel:* You are bound by secret contracts. Honor them.

THE SPIRIT

You are an aspect of another world, a creature beyond human comprehension. You may wish to return to your own place, but for now you are a stranger in the strange land of men.

- ↜ *Invoke:* Gain two dice when manipulating the forces of magic.
- ↜ *Compel:* You are not human. Remind them.

THE BEAST

You are a savage, an animal who can walk and speak as a man. You are not necessarily evil, but it is a rare beast who finds comfort in the hearts of his fellow men.

- ↜ *Invoke:* Gain two dice when intimidating others.
- ↜ *Compel:* A beast is a carrier of burdens. Suffer in silence, but grow resentful of your masters.

SLAVE

Despite your best efforts, you have been enslaved by another character in the Play. You must serve the letter of his or her law, but not the spirit.

- ↬ *Invoke:* Gain two dice when carrying out your master's orders.
- ↬ *Compel:* You hate your master. Twist orders to suit your interests.

BETROTHED

You are pledged to be married to another character in the Play. You may know little about your future spouse, but the impending marriage grows closer by the day.

- ↬ *Invoke:* Gain two dice when protecting your future mate.
- ↬ *Compel:* You aren't married yet. Flirt with another.

GUARDIAN

You are sworn to guard and protect and object, place, or person. You are unwavering in this oath, and it has come to define you and your view of the world.

- ↬ *Invoke:* Gain two dice when protecting your charge.
- ↬ *Compel:* You cannot abandon your post.

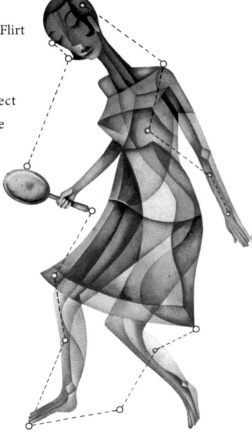

NEW PROPS

- Staff: Add one die when performing occult magic.
- Fan: Add one die when attempting to seduce another character.

NEW PLACES

ISLAND SET

A land lost in time and shrouded in mystery, the Island contains a heart of dark desire and plenty of fantastic adventure.

- Potential Places: Shipwrecked Beach, Bubbling Spring, Secret Oasis

PASTORAL SET

Far away from the land of courts and princes, the Pastoral is home to farmers and goatkeepers.

- Potential Places: Humble Cottage, Quiet Forest, Grassy Range

THE TEMPEST, A ROMANCE

The Tempest is Shakespeare's final play, a grand work that spans many locations and many years to tell the story of an exiled Duke who shames his enemies into renouncing their evil deeds. Like a Comedy, The Tempest works to heal the wrongs of the past with marriages and reconciliations that reunite old allies. Yet, there are some readers who view Prospero's actions as controlling and manipulative, and feel that he violates the free will that the other characters should have to make their own decisions.

  THE CAST

Alonso, King of Naples and ally of Antonio

- *Starting Part/Plot/Prop:* The Ruler, Father to Ferdinand, Crown
- "You cram these words into mine ears against the stomach of my sense."

Sebastian, Alonso's brother

- *Starting Part/Plot/Prop:* The Knight, Brother to Alonso, Sword
- "A pox o' your throat, you bawling, blasphemous, incharitable dog!"
- "I do; and surely it is a sleepy language and thou speak'st out of thy sleep."

Antonio, Duke of Milan

- *Starting Part/Plot/Prop:* The Ruler, Brother to Prospero, Coin
- "We all were sea-swallow'd, though some cast again."
- "The latter end of his commonwealth forgets the beginning."
- "Let's all sink with the king."

Ferdinand, Prince of Naples

- *Starting Part/Plot/Prop:* The Hero, Son of Alonso, Sword
- "There be some sports are painful, and their labour delight in them sets off."
- " I, beyond all limit of what else in the world do love, prize, honour you."

Gonzalo, an honest man from Naples

- *Starting Part/Plot/Prop:* The Knight, Friend to Prospero, Sword
- "Methinks he hath no drowning mark upon him; his complexion is perfect gallows."
- "Now would I give a thousand furlongs of sea for an acre of barren ground."

Prospero, the lord of the island

- *Starting Part/Plot/Prop:* The Magician, Father to Miranda, Staff
- "What see'st thou else in the dark backward and abysm of time?"
- "The strongest oaths are straw to th' fire i' the blood."

Miranda, the fair daughter of Prospero

- *Starting Part/Plot/Prop:* The Maiden, Daughter to Prospero, Fan
- "I am your wife, if you will marry me; if not, I'll die your maid."
- "I might call him a thing divine, for nothing natural I ever saw so noble."
- "O, wonder! How beauteous mankind is! O brave new world, that has such people in't!

Ariel, a spirit of the island

- *Starting Part/Plot/Prop:* The Spirit, Slave to Prospero, Lute
- "I will be correspondent to command, and do my spriting gently."
- "If of life you keep a care, shake off slumber, and beware. Awake, awake!"

Caliban, the former lord of the island

- *Starting Part/Plot/Prop:* The Beast, Slave to Prospero, Knife
- "This island's mine, by Sycorax my mother, which thou tak'st from me."
- "You taught me language, and my profit on't is, I know how to curse."

Act 1: Palace Set—Royal Quarters

Prospero explains to Miranda how his obsession with magic allowed his brother, Antonio, to usurp Prospero's dukedom and drive him out of Milan. Antonio was aided by King Alonso in his treachery, but Prospero and Miranda were able to escape with the help of Gonzalo, who gave them needed supplies. He tells her that they are blessed that the group of men who betrayed him have shipwrecked on the island. Prospero then puts Miranda to sleep, using magic, and summons forward Ariel to confirm that his plans to shipwreck his enemies on the island has been successful. He orders Ariel to fetch Ferdinand, son of Alonso, so that Miranda may fall in love with him. Miranda is smitten as soon as she sees the young prince, but Prospero, fearing that their love may not last if it is won too easily, insists the the boy is dangerous and imprisons him with magic.

Act 2: Island Set—Shipwrecked Beach

Alonso, Antonio, Gonzalo, and Sebastian, trapped on the other side of the island, search for Ferdinand. Ariel puts them most of them to sleep with magical music, leaving only Sebastian and Antonio awake. While the King sleeps, Antonio attempts to convince Sebastian to kill his brother and take the crown. Antonio agrees, but Ariel awakens the other men before the murder can occur. Antonio quickly constructs a story that justifies his drawn sword, but the King and his close advisors grow suspicious. Meanwhile, Caliban—Prospero's other slave on the island—plots to overthrow Prospero by taking his master's magic books and killing him.

Act 3: Palace Set—Servant Quarters

Ferdinand, trapped by Prospero's magic, does Caliban's chores, such as hauling wood. He does the work joyfully, thankful to be close to Miranda. Miranda, despite her father's orders not to talk to Ferdinand, joins him and eventually proposes marriage. Ferdinand accepts, and Prospero—overjoyed that his daughter has found love—rushes in to free

Ferdinand and celebrate the couple's happiness. He immediately blesses their marriage plans.

Act 4: Palace Set—Royal Quarters

Prospero calls upon spirits to perform a masque that will bless and entertain the new couple. When the masque is concluded, Ariel and Prospero set a trap for Caliban and his allies, leaving fancy clothes outside Prospero's estate. Caliban's party is distracted by the garments, and Ariel summons spirits to chase them away from Prospero's lands, scattering his allies and breaking the fledgling rebellion.

Act 5: Pastoral Set—Idyllic Grove

Ariel leads Alonso and his men to a grove where Prospero greets them. He chastises his betrayers for their treachery, but forgives them and reveals that Ferdinand is still alive. Alonso, overcome with joy to see him son again, apologizes for his actions, but Prospero demands only reconciliation and the restoration of his Dukedom. The men agree, and the party begins to prepare to sail back to Milan. Prospero concludes the play by breaking his staff and burning his books, renouncing magic forever.

GLOSSARY

Act: One of the five scenes a Troupe plays out in the course of playing *The Play's The Thing*. At the start of each Act, the Playwright provides a short synopsis of what is expected to occur.

Acting Chops: The statistics that describe an Actor's skill, broken into Logos, Pathos, and Ethos.

Acting Type: One of four types of Actors chosen by the Players at the start of the game. Each type has a different set of abilities.

Actor: The persona created by a Player for use in the game.

Character: The role an Actor wins through the casting process.

Comedy: A type of Shakespearean play typified by lowbrow humor and an affirmation of the social order through marriage.

Direction: A command that the Director may give an Actor based on his or her Actor Type.

Edit: A change to the Play proposed by the Actors.

Ethos: An Acting Chop that determines an Actor's ability to control the setting and props available in the Play.

Ham: The Acting Type for an over-the-top character Actor who attempts to steal the spotlight as often as possible.

History: A type of Shakespearean play that chronicles an English monarch's rise to (or fall from) power.

Ingénue: The Acting Type for the young and innocent Actor who wins over the audience with naiveté.

Lead: The Acting Type for the consummate professional who turns in an award-winning performance.

Logos: An Acting Chop that determines an Actor's ability to control the outcome of events in the Play.

Offstage Ability: A power—determined by the Character's Actor Type—that can only be used when the Character is offstage.

Onstage Ability: A power—determined by the Character's Actor Type—that can only be used when the Character is onstage.

Part: A formal role that an Actor must occupy on stage while playing his or her Character; it can be called upon to add dice to an Edit roll.

Pathos: An Acting Chop that determines an Actor's ability to alter the emotions and decisions of other Characters in the Play.

Place: A specific part of a Set that can be called upon to add a die to an Edit roll.

Playwright: The referee, storyteller, and overseer of the game session.

Plot: A relationship that an Actor must portray on stage while playing his or her Character; it can be called upon to add dice to an Edit roll.

Prop: An object that an Actor may bring on stage; it can be called upon to add a die to an Edit roll.

Script: One of the condensed synopses of a Shakespearean play for use with *The Play's The Thing*.

Set: An overall descriptor for the setting of the events that occur within an Act.

Story Points: An out-of-character currency that is used to activate powers or proposed Edits. Players receive story points for portraying their character in a Comedic, Tragic, or Historical way.

Tragedy: A type of Shakespearean play in which a tragic hero is undone by his own flaws, resulting in death for most of the cast.

Troupe: A group of Actors who play *The Play's The Thing* together.

Villain: The Acting Type for the Actor who is known for playing the evil and malicious malcontents of the Play.

Step 1: Create Actors (see page 20)

- Name your Actor
- Assign six points of Acting Chops (Logos, Pathos, Ethos)
- Select an Actor Type (Lead, Ham, Villain, or Ingénue)

Step 2: Cast the Play (see page 34)

- Hand out five story points to each Actor
- Offer up Characters with starting bid
- Actors bid up, pass on, or claim Characters
- Hand out Character lines to each Actor

Step 3: Set the Act (see page 48)

- Announce the Set and Place
- Select two Characters to start the Act
- Provide a synopsis of the Act

Step 4: Play the Act (see page 50)

- Run a freeform improvisational scene based on the synopsis
- Make Edits when the Actors want something in the play to change
- Repeat Step 3 for each new Act, ending with Act 5

Edit Mechanics (see page 52)

If a Player wants to make an Edit, he or she should spend a story point and yell "Cut!"

- *The Playwright can accept the Edit,* and return the story point, or can decline the Edit.
- *If the Player wants to Force the Edit,* The Playwright should determine the Edit's difficulty (Trivial, Minor, Major) which determines the Target Number (10, 15, or 20)
- The Player gathers dice, using the base of a Logos, Pathos, or Ethos score plus additional dice, and rolls all of them.
- If the total of the roll meets the Target Number, the Edit is Forced, and the Play continues.
- If the total does not meet the Target Number, the Edit fails, and the Play continues.

Element	Bonus	Cost
Part	2 dice	1 story point
Plot	2 dice	1 story point
Prop	1 die	free
Place	1 die	free

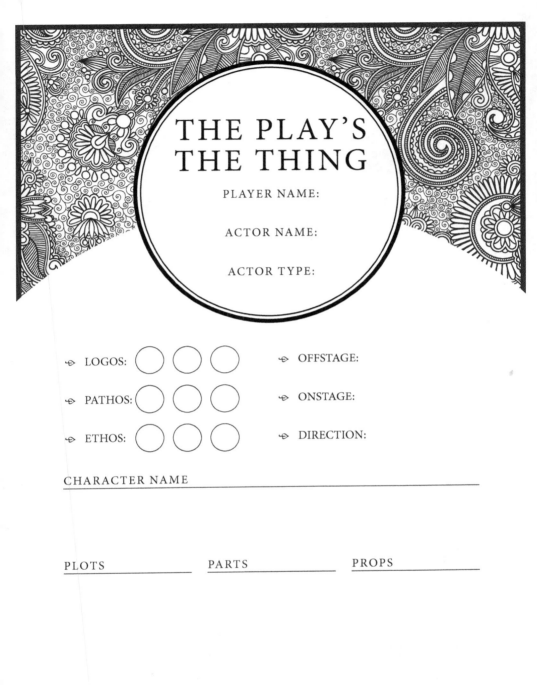

THE PLAY'S THE THING

PLAYER NAME:

ACTOR NAME:

ACTOR TYPE:

LOGOS: ◯ ◯ ◯   OFFSTAGE:

PATHOS: ◯ ◯ ◯   ONSTAGE:

ETHOS: ◯ ◯ ◯   DIRECTION:

CHARACTER NAME

PLOTS   PARTS   PROPS

SPARK

CHALLENGE YOUR BELIEFS

A STORYTELLING,
ROLEPLAYING
GAME

Are **you** clever enough?

Liven-up your event with one of six murder mysteries and find out!

CLEVER BY HALF PRODUCTIONS

Bring THE THEATRE to YOU

Most Likely to Decease
High school may be a pain, but reunions can be murder.

'Til Death Do Us Part
It's a fairytale wedding until the obnoxious groom collapses.

One Life to Lose
Murder hits the small screen at this Hollywood bash.

Sudden Death
You're front-row for the taping of a new game show!

Murder of Convention
Play host to ShenCon 1, the sci-fi & fantasy convention.

Mountain of Crime
The Ntl. Crime Syndicate may be looking for a new Don.

interactive on demand live theatre.

Producing family-friendly Murder Mystery Theatre that is 100% portable and original since 2005. Browse and book our shows online.

visit us online at
www.cleverbyhalf.com

THE
CONGLOMERAT
PRESENTS

HANNOVER H spielt!

THE
TRADITIONAL GERMAN
GAMING CONVENTION
WHERE

**THE PLAY IS
ALWAYS THE THING**

— & —

Auf den Inseln an der Küste

THE ATMOSPHERIC
ANNUAL GATHERING
OF FRIENDS & FANS
OF GOOD GAMING

CPSIA information can be obtained
at www.ICGtesting.com
Printed in the USA
FSHW020447070321
79127FS